P9-CMV-440

Crazy Easy VEGAN DESSERTS

75 FAST, SIMPLE, **OVER-THE TOP-TREATS** THAT WILL ROCK YOUR WORLD!

Heather Saffer

STERLING EPICURE

New York

STERLING EPICURE
New York

An Imprint of Sterling Publishing Co., Inc.
1166 Avenue of the Americas
New York, NY 10036

ISBN 978-1-4549-2674-0

Distributed in Canada by Sterling Publishing Co., Inc.
c/o Canadian Manda Group, 664 Annette Street
Toronto, Ontario M6S 2C8, Canada
Distributed in the United Kingdom by GMC Distribution Services
Castle Place, 166 High Street, Lewes, East Sussex BN7 1XU, England
Distributed in Australia by NewSouth Books
45 Beach Street, Coogee NSW 2034, Australia

For information about custom editions, special sales,
and premium and corporate purchases, please contact
Sterling Special Sales at 800-805-5489 or specialsales@sterlingpublishing.com.

Manufactured in China

2 4 6 8 10 9 7 5 3 1

sterlingpublishing.com

Cover design by Elizabeth Mihaltse Lindy
Photography by Bill Milne
Food styling by Diane Vezza

A complete list of image credits appears on page 126.

DEDICATION

To Donald, my best friend, sassy fur ball,
and greatest traveling companion.
Your love, spunk, and adventurous antics
make my life so awesomely sweet.

CONTENTS

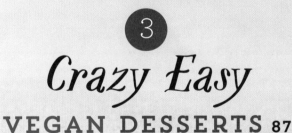

INTRODUCTION

My dessert journey began as a kid. I remember giggling with friends in the lunchroom while feasting on soft chocolate cookies sandwiched with creamy fudge frosting. At the end of the day, I would hop off the school bus and rush into my babysitter's house, eager to see what cookie concoction awaited me. Desserts appeared during those best of times—playing kickball with the neighborhood kids after school and on Saturday afternoons after grocery shopping with my mom. Dessert meant fun, playfulness, freedom. I remember dessert being the fun-filled sweet surprise in the middle and at the end of each day.

But truth be told, no one in my family ever baked. I grew up on packaged snack cakes and store-bought cookies, not even knowing what *vegan* meant.

So how did I become the author of a vegan dessert cookbook? Let me take a step back.

In 2009, I decided to teach myself how to bake. I went to the school of Google and YouTube and graduated by opening a create-your-own cupcake bakery in New York. Shortly thereafter, I proved my cupcake-baking skills by winning the TV competition *Cupcake Wars*. As lines formed out the door and around the block for my decadent cupcakes, I switched my focus to frosting and wrote my first cookbook, *The Dollop Book of Frosting*. It was around that time I learned that all those snack cakes I grew up loving were the cause of my lifelong stomach and digestion issues, and thus I cut gluten and dairy out of my diet. As my gut health cleared up, my new mission was also clarified: reinvent the desserts and snacks that were part of my fondest memories as gluten-free, dairy-free, vegan, and all-around better.

My mission began by veganizing my first love—frosting. So I created a line of vegan, gluten-free, non-GMO frostings, which is now carried in more than 600 retail stores nationwide. To my delight, Dollop Gourmet frosting was a hit, especially with the investors on the hit show *Shark Tank*!

Next, I continued with my mission of veganizing and healthifying America's favorite sweet snacks by creating Dollop Dunkers, a line of cookie and frosting snack packs, so that dessert lovers everywhere can have a fun vegan treat anytime they please.

So, as you can see, if anyone knows desserts, it's me. And if anyone needs them to be super easy to make because they have no time to make them, it's totally me.

But I have a secret: I don't like typical vegan desserts. The hard-to-find ingredients I've never heard of. The 10,000 steps it takes to create one batch of cookies. The gross smell when I open a can of coconut milk (seriously, you don't smell that?).

When I see a recipe for a dessert that calls for weird ingredients like arrowroot powder, xylitol, and raw cashews that must be soaked for five hours and then blended and hung out to dry on a warm summer day while an easy wind blows, I'm thinking the recipe writer lives on a commune and has lost her mind.

First, who has time to wait for cashews to soak for five hours? I'll have eaten three cookies, a brownie, and a slice of chocolate cake by the time those nuts are ready to be made into whatever flavorless bar/cheesecake/cookie they're supposed to be.

Second, raw cashews? Black beans? Tofu? Are we making desserts or appetizers for a Super Bowl party? Where is my chocolatey, custard-filled Boston Cream Cake (page 54)? Or

warm Apple Pie Blondies (page 29) dusted with cinnamon sugar? I mean, let's get dessert back to dessert here, friends! Just because we're vegan and believe in honoring life doesn't mean our desserts need to be lifeless. Who's with me?

I'm not sure at what point vegan came to be equated with dull (maybe it's the lifeless component?), but I'm here to change that. Stat.

In the following pages, you'll find all sorts of your favorite desserts reinvented as vegan and gluten-free. These desserts are easy. So easy. Very, very easy. I really can't say it enough. They're *easy*. If you're afraid of eating vegan, I'm here to snap you out of your fear. By using ingredients you know and love, and by making the desserts so easy that a three-year-old can make them, I've given you no excuse not to get into that kitchen, tie on a hot little apron, and put some fun in your day with very easy vegan desserts. Plus, these desserts are not just easy, they're divinely delicious. From ooey-gooey to crispy-crunchy to tender and chewy, the vegan desserts I've crafted especially for you in this book taste downright mind-blowing. Get ready to lick your fingers clean through all 128 pages of yum.

EASY TIPS AND VERY EASY TRICKS

Making vegan desserts is easier than you think, and I'm here to help. My first order of business is to provide you with a list of tips, tricks, and necessary ingredient purchases to get your vegan baking adventure off the ground and on its way to intergalactic glory.

Your first questions are probably, "But what about eggs? And milk? How do I replace those?" Here's the breakdown.

EGGS

Eggs add structure, moisture, and stability in baking. There are a few simple substitutions for eggs in vegan baking. In this book, I've already suggested the egg replacements to use for each recipe, but feel free to play around and choose a different one if you'd like.

◆ UNSWEETENED APPLESAUCE Use 1/4 cup unsweetened applesauce to replace each egg.

◆ FLAX SEEDS Use 1 tablespoon ground flax seeds plus 3 tablespoons water to replace each egg. Stir together the ground flax and water and let sit until the mixture thickens, 10 to 15 minutes.

◆ CHIA SEEDS Use 1 tablespoon ground chia seeds plus 3 tablespoons water to replace each egg. Stir together the ground chia and water and let sit until the mixture thickens, 10 to 15 minutes.

◆ AQUAFABA, AKA CHICKPEA WATER Use 3 tablespoons liquid from a can of chickpeas to replace each egg.

◆ BANANA Use ¼ cup mashed ripe banana to replace each egg.

MILK

There's a vast array of nondairy milks on the market now. Pick your favorite—almond, soy, cashew . . . just make sure you choose unsweetened since we're adding sugar to the recipes already.

BUTTERMILK

To make a vegan version of tangy buttermilk, put 1 tablespoon apple cider vinegar or lemon juice in a 1-cup measure and fill to the brim the nondairy milk of your choice. Let it sit for about 5 minutes to thicken and become tangy before adding to your recipe. Easy!

BUTTER

You'll see my choices of butter substitutes throughout the recipes. In most instances, I prefer to use sustainably sourced palm shortening (I like Earth Balance® brand) or refined coconut oil. I always make sure the palm oil I use is sustainable and certified by either the Roundtable on Sustainable Palm Oil or the Rainforest Alliance. You can generally find this information on the company's website.

Other options are vegan margarine or unrefined coconut oil. I prefer to use refined coconut oil over unrefined coconut oil because refined has zero coconut flavor. As much as I may like coconut, I don't want all my desserts tasting like it! In some recipes, shortening just works better than coconut oil as coconut oil tends to break down more quickly and, if not used correctly, can lead to an oily finished product.

FLOUR

Since I can't eat gluten, any time I mention flour in this book I'm referring to gluten-free flour. I've only tested these recipes with gluten-free flour, but if you feel determined to try making them with regular flour, I won't try to stop you. I can't promise it will work out, but I'm sure you'll let me know if it doesn't. My favorite brand is Bob's Red Mill 1-to-1 Gluten-Free Flour. All brands have different combinations of flours and binding agents so they may react differently, but my fantastic recipe testers tested most of these recipes using a variety of different gluten-free flours, so you should be good to go. Just make sure you always buy one that is labeled "1-to-1," as it is a direct replacement for regular flour.

SUGAR

Some granulated sugars, brown sugars, and powdered sugars are bleached using bone char from cows, which means it's not vegan. You'll want to make sure you're buying bone char–free sugar if that's a problem for you. A quick Google search will lead you to those sugar brands that don't use bone char. Generally speaking, if you're using organic or non-

GMO sugar, you're safe, but I suggest double-checking just in case.

VANILLA

When I call for vanilla, I mean *pure* vanilla extract. Don't use the fake stuff. You're better than that.

PROBLEM SOLVING

Vegan gluten-free baking can *sometimes* turn out different from conventional baking, I'm not going to lie. But that's why I'm here! I want to help you do everything possible to make sure your desserts turn out spectacularly every single time.

TIP #1 Have fun! This is my top dessert-making/eating rule. If you're not having fun, pour yourself a drink or a tall glass of nondairy milk, take a break, and center yourself. Dessert should be fun! Get in the groove, pump some jams, and get ready to party down for dessert.

TIP #2 Above all else, make sure you do not overmix your batters. Overmixing will cause heavy, dense cakes. If that's your style, mix away. If not, light touch on that mixer speed, hulk: 1 to 2 minutes should do you just fine.

TIP #3 Don't use frozen fruits. I know it may be hard to resist making that Mixed Berry Banana Cake in the dead of winter, but unless you can score fresh berries, you'll just have to wait. Frozen berries contain too much water and mess with the consistency of the cake. You'll be eating soup cake in front of your fireplace if you go the frozen route.

TIP #4 If the center of your cake is runny, keep baking it until a toothpick inserted into the center comes out with moist crumbs attached.

TIP #5 Let cookies cool slightly before removing them from the cookie sheet. They'll fall apart if your patience wears thin and you dig in too soon.

TIP #6 *Have fun!!!*

DISCLAIMER I'm not going to repeat "vegan" prior to every listing of milk, chocolate chips, butter, frosting, and so on. I'm just going to assume at this point you understand this is a vegan cookbook and thus every ingredient you choose should be vegan. You're a smart reader, I just know it! Okay, let's get started!

Easy VEGAN DESSERTS

Now I know this book is called *Crazy Easy Vegan Desserts*, but we're going to start with "Easy" and work our way to "Crazy, Easy." Don't fret, these first recipes, while made entirely from scratch, are still incredibly simple and accessible. And believe me, these recipes *will* impress. From lightly sweetened Powdered Blueberry Donuts that are the perfect breakfast treat to decadent, sticky-sweet Bourbon Pecan Pie Bars, the recipes in this section are simple, satisfying, and so worth whipping up right this minute. Get to it, dollface!

CINNAMON SUGAR COOKIES

Makes 12 to 18 cookies

I hated cinnamon as a child. Crazy, right? I was a crazy child for sure. But more about that later. Cinnamon is healthy(!), and it adds that little something special to these sugar cookies, which are moist, slightly crumbly, and just cinnamon-y enough to be a real crowd pleaser.

● ₀ ●● ●

1½ cups gluten-free flour

½ cup plus ⅓ cup granulated sugar, divided

½ teaspoon baking soda

¼ teaspoon salt

½ cup unsweetened applesauce

½ cup vegetable oil

1 tablespoon vanilla extract

1½ teaspoons cinnamon

1 Preheat the oven to 375°F. Line a baking sheet with parchment paper.

2 In a medium bowl, whisk together the flour, ½ cup sugar, baking soda, and salt. In a separate bowl, mix together the applesauce, oil, and vanilla. Slowly add the flour mixture while mixing on medium speed until well combined. Refrigerate the dough until firm enough to roll, 10 to 20 minutes.

3 In a small bowl, stir together the cinnamon and the remaining one-third cup sugar.

4 Shape dough into 1 inch balls and roll in the cinnamon-sugar mixture to coat. Flatten each ball slightly. Arrange balls on the lined baking sheet and bake until the edges begin to brown, about 10 minutes.

note
✶ ✶ ✶ ✶ ✶ ✶ ✶ ✶ ✶ ✶ ✶ ✶
Consider making extra cinnamon-sugar mixture and sprinkling it on your pancakes in the morning. Yum!

PUMPKIN OATMEAL
CHOCOLATE CHIP COOKIES

Makes 12 to 16 cookies

When September rolls around and your friends and officemates do nothing but wax poetic about their love for pumpkin, you'll be glad to have this tricked-out oatmeal cookie recipe in your back pocket. With just the right sprinkling of chocolate chips and a touch of cinnamon, the pumpkin is the true star here. Only make these if you're ready for your boss to bow down to you all October long.

2 cups gluten-free flour

1 cup rolled oats

1 teaspoon baking soda

½ teaspoon baking powder

½ teaspoon salt

½ teaspoon cinnamon

¾ cup palm shortening

1 cup packed light brown sugar

¼ cup granulated sugar

¾ cup canned pumpkin

2 tablespoons unsweetened applesauce

½ teaspoon vanilla extract

1 cup chocolate chips

1 Preheat the oven to 375°F. Line a baking sheet with parchment paper.

2 In a medium bowl, mix together the flour, oats, baking soda, baking powder, salt, and cinnamon. In the bowl of a stand mixer, beat the shortening with the sugars until creamed together. Add the pumpkin, applesauce, and vanilla and mix until well combined. Slowly add the flour mixture and continue mixing until well combined. Add the chocolate chips and mix until well dispersed.

3 Drop tablespoon-size balls of dough on the lined baking sheet. Flatten each ball slightly. Bake until the edges begin to turn golden, 10 to 12 minutes. Remove from the oven and let cool.

note

Spread softened vegan vanilla ice cream or salted caramel ice cream between two of these pumpkin cookies and you'll be chomping down on one killer ice cream sandwich.

CHOCOLATE CHIP
MACADAMIA NUT COOKIES

Makes 12 to 16 cookies

One time when I was invited to speak to a group of businesspeople, I began by telling the story of how my entry into the wide world of desserts and business came about. Halfway through my story, the man who invited me to speak leaned over to me and asked, "Do you realize how ridiculous this sounds as it's coming out of your mouth?" to which we all laughed. My story is pretty nutty, if you ever get the chance to hear it! And that's not even including the details. Next book: a memoir. Mark my words. Until then, read Betty White's memoir (she's grand) and whip up a batch of these scrumptiously nutty chocolate chip cookies.

• • •• •

2¼ cups gluten-free flour

1 teaspoon baking soda

¼ teaspoon salt

1 cup palm shortening

½ cup granulated sugar

½ cup packed light brown sugar

¼ cup unsweetened almond milk

1 teaspoon vanilla extract

8 ounces chocolate chips

4 ounces macadamia nuts, chopped

note
Swap out the macadamia nuts for walnuts, pecans, or even peanuts!

1 Preheat the oven to 350°F. Line a baking sheet with parchment paper.

2 In a small bowl, whisk together the flour, baking soda, and salt. In a large bowl, cream together the shortening and sugars. Add the almond milk and vanilla and mix until combined. Slowly add the flour mixture, scraping down the sides of the bowl as needed. Fold in the chocolate chips and macadamia nuts. Refrigerate the dough for 10 to 15 minutes.

3 Scoop tablespoon-size balls onto the lined baking sheet. Flatten each ball slightly. Bake until the edges begin to turn golden, 8 to 10 minutes. Remove from the oven and let cool for a few minutes, then transfer to a wire rack to cool completely.

SUGAR COOKIE FRUIT "PIZZAS"

Makes 8 to 12 "pizzas"

People can't seem to understand why I don't crave pizza like every other normal human on the planet. I dunno, but pizza has never been my kryptonite. But turn that idea into a sugar cookie covered in creamy frosting and topped with vibrant fruit? You'll have a "pizza" my heart in no time.

• • • •

1¾ cups gluten-free flour

1½ teaspoons cornstarch

½ teaspoon baking soda

1 teaspoon baking powder

½ teaspoon salt

½ cup vegan butter, softened

½ cup packed light brown sugar

¼ cup granulated sugar

¼ cup unsweetened applesauce

2 teaspoons vanilla extract

1 to 2 teaspoons water or unsweetened nondairy milk

1 (12-ounce) jar Dollop Gourmet Madagascar Vanilla vegan frosting

½ cup fresh strawberries, chopped

½ cup fresh blueberries

½ cup chopped kiwi

note

✳ ✳ ✳ ✳ ✳ ✳ ✳ ✳ ✳ ✳ ✳ ✳

The more colorful the fruit, the better! Having a party? Set out plain baked cookies, bowls of frosting, and dishes of chopped fruit and let your guests decorate their own pizzas. This also makes a perfect after-school activity and snack.

1 In a small bowl, whisk together the flour, cornstarch, baking soda, baking powder, and salt. In a medium bowl, beat the vegan butter with a mixer until creamy. Add the sugars and beat for 1 minute. Add the applesauce and vanilla and mix until incorporated. Slowly add the flour mixture, mixing until incorporated, taking care not to overmix. Add enough water or nondairy milk until a soft dough comes together. Freeze the dough, covered, for 15 minutes.

2 Preheat the oven to 350°F. Line two baking sheets with parchment paper.

3 Roll heaping tablespoon-size scoops of dough into balls and arrange 2 inches apart on the lined baking sheets. Flatten each ball slightly into a disk. Bake until slightly golden, 10 to 12 minutes. Remove from the oven and let cool completely before frosting.

4 Spread a layer of frosting on each cookie and decorate with the strawberries, blueberries, and kiwi. Serve at once.

ZUCCHINI OATMEAL COOKIES

Makes about 2 dozen cookies

I brought these cookies to my therapist. I had been on some sort of obsessive zucchini cookie-making streak, and it was the third week in a row that I had told her about these healthy, veggie-packed cookies. (I wonder what that said about my state of mind in those days . . . nutty baker hunched over the kitchen counter, wildly shredding zucchini late into the night.) But these cookies are that good, and with all that zucchini, you're practically eating a salad. So go ahead—indulge. And make a few extra for your therapist while you're at it.

1 tablespoon ground flax seeds

3 tablespoons water

1 cup gluten-free flour

1 teaspoon baking soda

1 teaspoon ground cinnamon

½ teaspoon salt

⅛ teaspoon ground cloves

⅛ teaspoon ground nutmeg

¾ cup packed dark brown sugar

¼ cup flavored applesauce (I like strawberry)

1 teaspoon vanilla extract

½ teaspoon rum extract

1 cup shredded zucchini

2 cups rolled oats

½ cup semisweet chocolate chips

1 Preheat the oven to 350°F. Line a baking sheet with parchment paper.

2 In a small bowl, stir together the ground flax seeds and water and let sit until thickened, 5 to 10 minutes.

3 In a bowl, whisk together the flour, baking soda, cinnamon, salt, cloves, and nutmeg. In a large mixing bowl, mix together the brown sugar, applesauce, the flaxseed mixture, vanilla, and rum extract. Add the shredded zucchini and mix until combined. Slowly add the flour mixture and mix until just combined. Stir in the oats and chocolate chips.

4 Drop tablespoon-size scoops of cookie dough onto the lined baking sheet. Bake until golden brown, 10 to 12 minutes. Transfer the cookies to wire racks to cool completely.

LEMON CHIA COCONUT BARS

Makes 9 to 12 bars

I heard through the grapevine that my great-grandmother used to make the most wonderful lemon chiffon pie. She didn't pass down her baking skills to anyone else in the family, so I never actually tasted this heirloom pie, but the stories make it sound truly divine. Inspired by my great-grandmother Momo Esther's pie, I created these sweet-tart bars. The crispness of the chia seeds and the tang of the lemon pair beautifully with the chewy coconut to make a truly delightful treat—as delightful as I've heard Momo Esther used to be. Here's to you, Momo. Hopefully I'm doing your baking heart justice.

BARS

2 tablespoons ground chia seeds

6 tablespoons water

Finely grated zest of ½ lemon

2 tablespoons fresh lemon juice

½ cup palm shortening

¾ cup gluten-free flour

¾ cup granulated sugar

¼ teaspoon salt

¼ cup unsweetened grated coconut

LEMON COCONUT GLAZE

½ cup powdered sugar

2 tablespoons unsweetened shredded coconut

1 tablespoon fresh lemon juice

1 Preheat the oven to 350°F. Line an 8-inch-square baking pan with parchment paper.

2 In a small bowl, mix the chia seeds with the water and let sit until thickened, 10 to 15 minutes. Add the lemon zest and juice. Set aside.

3 In a large bowl, beat the shortening until softened. Add the flour, sugar, and salt and continue mixing. Add the chia mixture and mix until well combined. Fold in the coconut.

4 Pour the batter into the baking pan and bake until puffed, about 25 minutes. Remove from the oven and let cool.

5 To make the glaze, stir together the powdered sugar, coconut, and lemon juice until a smooth glaze forms. Drizzle over the cooled bars before serving.

> **note**
> ＊＊＊＊＊＊＊＊＊＊＊＊＊
> Sprinkle additional chia seeds over
> the glaze if you want a little more
> crunch and superfood fiber.

RASPBERRY CRUMBLE BARS

Makes 9 to 12 bars

When my first cupcake business crumbled at the hands of a general manager I had brought on, I initially thought my life was over. But that's when I learned the powerful perseverance that lay within me. I picked myself up, kicked him to prison, and launched Dollop, my vehicle to success. I took a life-changing moment that started out sour and promptly turned it sweet. The lesson here is that even the crumbiest of experiences can have the sweetest endings. Just like these Raspberry Crumble Bars—oaty, fruity bars that fall apart on your plate yet are so perfectly sweet. Make these to remind you how good life can be.

1 cup gluten-free flour
¼ teaspoon baking soda
¼ teaspoon salt
1 cup rolled oats
½ cup packed light brown sugar
½ cup coconut oil, softened
1 teaspoon vanilla extract
¾ cup raspberry jam

> ### note
> Try serving this warm as a crumble with spoons and vegan ice cream. Yum!

1 Preheat the oven to 350°F. Line an 8-inch-square baking pan with parchment paper.

2 In a large bowl, whisk together the flour, baking soda, and salt. Add the oats and brown sugar and continue mixing. Add the coconut oil and vanilla and mix until just moistened, taking care not to overmix.

3 Spread 2⅓ cups of the oat mixture into the bottom of the pan, pressing firmly. Bake until the edges begin to brown, 10 to 15 minutes. Remove from the oven and let cool slightly.

4 Spread the jam evenly over the oat mixture, coming almost to the edge but not quite. Sprinkle the remaining oat mixture evenly over the top, pressing down slightly to adhere. Bake until the top starts to turn golden brown, 25 to 30 minutes. Remove from the oven and refrigerate for 1 to 2 hours to firm up before cutting into squares.

LEMON CREAM CHEESE THUMBPRINT COOKIES

Makes about 16 cookies

When I was growing up Jewish in New York, bagels with cream cheese were the *thing*. Standing in line at the bagel shop, the smell of hot fresh bagels permeating the air, I'd watch intently as the young guy behind the counter sliced my bagel in half with a giant serrated knife and plopped an ice cream scoop-size ball of cream cheese directly in the center of one half. With a metal spatula, he'd spread the cream cheese quickly over each half as it began to melt, finally sandwiching the bagel and wrapping it in paper. But enough about bagels, we've got cookies to make! These lemony cream cheese thumbprint cookies, with their chewy texture and bright strawberry jam dropped cleanly in the center, remind me of those warm cream cheese–covered bagel days.

• • •

½ cup palm shortening

2 ounces (¼ cup) cream cheese, softened

½ cup granulated sugar

2 tablespoons unsweetened applesauce

2 tablespoons fresh lemon juice

¼ teaspoon vanilla extract

1¼ cups gluten-free flour

Pinch of salt

3 tablespoons strawberry jam

1 Preheat the oven to 350°F. Line a baking sheet with parchment paper.

2 In a medium bowl, mix together the shortening, cream cheese, and sugar until fluffy. Add the applesauce, lemon juice, and vanilla, and continue mixing. Add the flour and salt and mix until well blended. Chill the dough in the freezer for 10 minutes.

3 Arrange tablespoon-size balls of dough on the baking sheet. Using the back of a spoon or your thumb, make an indentation in the center of each ball. Drop about ½ teaspoon strawberry jam in the center of each cookie. Bake the cookies until the bottoms begin to brown, about 15 minutes. Let cool before removing from the baking sheet.

CHERRY PISTACHIO COOKIES

Makes 12 to 16 cookies

I just love pistachios. They have such a unique flavor, unmatched by any other nut, and they pair so well with other flavors, especially cherries. These shortbread-style cookies loaded with dried cherries and pistachios are a real treat and a breeze to make.

• •• •

1 cup vegan butter

½ cup powdered sugar

1½ teaspoons vanilla extract

1 teaspoon pistachio extract (optional)

1¾ cups gluten-free flour

¼ teaspoon salt

2 tablespoons unsweetened almond milk

¾ cup dried cherries, chopped

⅔ cup shelled pistachios, chopped

1 In a medium bowl, cream together the vegan butter and sugar. Add the vanilla and pistachio extract, if using, and mix until combined. Slowly add the flour and salt and mix until large clumps form. Add the almond milk and mix until well combined. Fold in the cherries and pistachios.

2 Form the dough into a compact 2-inch-thick log, wrap tightly, and chill in the fridge for 1 to 2 hours.

3 Preheat the oven to 325°F. Line a baking sheet with parchment paper.

4 Carefully slice the log into ¼-inch-thick slices and place on the baking sheet. Bake until the tops start to brown, 10 to 15 minutes. Remove from the oven and let cool slightly before removing from the baking sheet.

note

Make sure to tightly press the dough into a log before chilling or it will fall apart when you slice it. Use those muscles!

BOURBON PECAN PIE BARS

Makes 9 to 12 bars

I have the world's worst memory, especially when it comes to books and movies. I can't tell you how many times I've rented a movie only to realize 30 minutes in that I've already seen it. When people try to quote movies to me? Forget about it. There's one exception though, and that's a line from *When Harry Met Sally*. No, it's not the line you're thinking of, you dirty mind. It's when Harry is talking in a funny voice to Sally and says, "Waiter, there's too much pepper in my paprikash. But I would be proud to partake in your pecan pieeeee. Pecan pieeeee. Pecan pieeeeee." Why this is the one line from any movie that I can quote is beyond me, but every time I think of it I get a hankering for pecan pieeeee. These Bourbon Pecan Pie Bars are the perfect cure for that hankering. Ooey-gooey and sticky-sweet, these portable little bites truly hit the spot.

● ˌ●˙● ●

FOR THE CRUST
½ cup vegan butter
1½ cups gluten-free flour
⅓ cup granulated sugar
¼ teaspoon salt
½ teaspoon vanilla extract

FOR THE FILLING
⅓ cup packed light brown sugar
¼ cup granulated sugar
4 tablespoons vegan butter
¼ cup maple syrup
3 tablespoons bourbon
2 cups pecans, roughly chopped

note
If you want to make these nonalcoholic, replace the bourbon with 2 tablespoons unsweetened almond milk.

1 Preheat the oven to 350°F. Line an 8-inch-square baking pan with parchment paper.

2 To make the crust, combine the vegan butter, flour, sugar, salt, and vanilla in a food processor and pulse until crumbly. Press the mixture firmly into the prepared baking pan and bake until golden brown, 20 to 25 minutes. Remove from the oven to cool while you make the filling.

3 To make the filling, combine the sugars, vegan butter, maple syrup, and bourbon in a medium saucepan and bring to a boil over medium heat. Reduce the heat and simmer for 5 minutes, stirring occasionally so it doesn't burn. Remove from the heat and stir in the pecans.

4 Spread the filling evenly over the crust. Let cool, then transfer to the refrigerator overnight for the filling to set. Once completely set, cut into bars.

LEMON MERINGUES

Makes about 50 cookies

I'm hooked on *The Golden Girls*. Many nights, I pour myself a glass (or two) of red wine, pull out some freshly baked dessert, and stream two or three episodes. I often watched the show growing up, but since I have such a horrible memory, it's like every episode is brand new when I watch it now. The gals sure do crack me up! Sophia is a spitting image of my grandma, albeit much shorter, and Blanche is so much like my mom's best friend, Mary, that I can't help but smile while I watch. I've always loved spending time with older ladies, so watching them on TV makes me feel right at home. These little lemon meringues are a lot like the Golden Girls—sweet yet tart golden bites of goodness.

1 (15-ounce) can sodium-free chickpeas, undrained

¼ teaspoon cream of tartar

¾ cup granulated sugar

1 teaspoon freshly grated lemon zest, plus more for decorating

1 tablespoon fresh lemon juice

> ### note
> Try adding vanilla extract and mini chocolate chips, instead of lemon, to these meringues.

1 Preheat the oven to 210°F. Line a baking sheet with parchment paper.

2 Measure out ½ cup liquid from the can of chickpeas. Reserve the chickpeas for another use (perhaps hummus for dinner?). Pour the liquid into a medium bowl and add the cream of tartar. Beat with an electric mixer until soft peaks form. Add the sugar very slowly, beating constantly, and continue to beat until glossy peaks form, about 20 minutes. Beat in the lemon zest and juice until incorporated.

3 Spoon the mixture into a piping bag and pipe 1-inch rounds on the baking sheet. Sprinkle with additional lemon zest for decoration, if you'd like.

4 Bake until the meringues are firm and can be peeled easily from the parchment paper, about 1½ hours. Let cool completely.

APPLE PIE BLONDIES

Makes 9 to 12 blondies

You guys, listen. I made this recipe and ate the whole pan in two days. *Two. Days.* It's almost kinda sorta healthy though. Coconut oil! An apple! Applesauce! It's like a giant pan of health. Just heed my warning: make sure you're prepared to hit the gym the day after making these cinnamon-scented blondies because you won't be able to refrain from eating more than six pieces in one sitting. Want to do a double at the gym? Try serving these with a scoop of vegan vanilla ice cream and an extra sprinkling of cinnamon to make your apple pie dreams come alive.

• • • •

1 cup gluten-free flour

1¼ teaspoons ground cinnamon, divided

1 teaspoon baking powder

¼ teaspoon salt

¼ cup coconut oil, melted

¼ cup plus 1 teaspoon granulated sugar, divided

¼ cup packed light brown sugar

¼ cup unsweetened applesauce

1 teaspoon vanilla extract

1 medium apple, such as Fuji, finely chopped

note

Try other apple varieties for slightly different flavors. Macintosh, Granny Smith, Gala, Empire, Jonagold . . . there are so many, you'll never get bored.

1 Preheat the oven to 350°F. Spray an 8-inch-square baking pan with nonstick cooking spray.

2 In a small bowl, whisk together flour, ¼ teaspoon cinnamon, baking powder, and salt. In the bowl of a stand mixer, beat together the coconut oil, ¼ cup granulated sugar, and brown sugar. Add the applesauce and vanilla and mix until blended, scraping down the sides of the bowl as needed. Slowly add the flour mixture and mix until well combined. Add the chopped apples and mix until evenly dispersed.

3 Spread the batter evenly into the prepared pan. In a small bowl, mix together the remaining 1 teaspoon cinnamon and 1 teaspoon sugar. Sprinkle the mixture evenly over the batter. Bake until a toothpick inserted in the center comes out clean, 25 to 30 minutes.

4 Cut into squares and serve warm.

COOKIES AND CREAM DONUTS

Makes 6 donuts

There were often donuts in my house. My mom would go to Jazzercise in the morning and come home with donuts from the local shop, including a giant coffee roll for herself, that she slowly savored while sipping coffee at the kitchen island and reading the paper. I preferred chocolate-glazed donut holes and white frosting–filled donuts, which I would eat by nibbling all around the edge first, saving the giant mound of frosting for last. These donuts are a combination of my two faves: chocolate cake donuts frosted with creamy vanilla frosting, all topped with crushed chocolate cookies. Donuts don't get much better than this!

• • • •

1½ teaspoons distilled white vinegar

½ cup unsweetened almond milk

1 cup gluten-free flour

¼ cup unsweetened dark cocoa powder

½ teaspoon baking soda

Pinch of salt

½ cup granulated sugar

¼ cup unsweetened applesauce

2 teaspoons coconut oil, melted

1 teaspoon vanilla extract

12 vegan crunchy chocolate cookies, crushed

1 (12-ounce) jar Dollop Gourmet Madagascar Vanilla vegan frosting

note

Instead of frosting the tops of the donuts, try slicing each one in half and frosting the middles to create a donut sandwich. Spread a bit more frosting on the top of the donut sandwich and sprinkle with cookie crumbs.

1 Preheat the oven to 350°F. Spray a donut pan with nonstick cooking spray.

2 Pour the vinegar into a ½ cup measure. Add enough almond milk to come to the brim. Let sit until slightly thickened, 5 to 10 minutes.

3 In a small bowl, whisk together the flour, cocoa powder, baking soda, and salt. In a large bowl, mix together the sugar, applesauce, coconut oil, and vanilla. Slowly add the flour mixture and mix until smooth. Add the almond milk mixture and continue mixing for 1 minute more. Add half of the crushed cookies and mix until just combined.

4 Scoop the batter into the prepared donut pan, filling three-quarters of the way full. Bake until a toothpick inserted into the center comes out clean, 10 to 15 minutes. Let cool before frosting.

5 Microwave the uncovered frosting jar for 5-second intervals, stirring in between, until soft. Gently frost the top of each donut. Sprinkle the remaining crushed cookies over the donuts.

CHOCOLATE CRUNCH BROWNIES

Makes 9 to 12 brownies

My favorite desserts have multiple layers, textures, and dimensions. Chewy bottoms, crunchy crusts, melty middles. . . . However you layer it, the greater the juxtaposition of textures, the better. Even when sticking with one flavor, like chocolate, you can still create a really delightful and surprising treat just by adding different textures. Take one bite of these crunchy-chewy-soft brownies and you'll see what I mean.

● ●●●

1 cup gluten-free flour
⅔ cup unsweetened cocoa powder
½ teaspoon baking powder
½ teaspoon salt
1 cup unsweetened applesauce
½ cup granulated sugar
4 tablespoons coconut oil, melted
⅔ cup chocolate chips
1 cup dark chocolate, finely chopped
3 cups Rice Chex™ cereal, crushed

1 Preheat the oven to 350°F. Lightly spray an 8-inch-square baking pan with nonstick cooking spray.

2 In a bowl, whisk together the flour, cocoa powder, baking powder, and salt. In a medium bowl, mix together the applesauce, sugar, and coconut oil until blended. Slowly add the flour mixture and mix until well combined, about 2 minutes. Add the chocolate chips and mix until evenly dispersed.

3 Spread the batter evenly in the baking pan and bake until a toothpick inserted in the center comes out with moist crumbs attached, 25 to 30 minutes.

4 In a medium bowl, melt the chopped chocolate in the microwave at 30-second intervals, stirring in between. Continue until completely melted, being careful not to burn the chocolate. Add the crushed cereal and toss to coat.

5 Spread the chocolate cereal mix evenly over the top of the just baked brownies and let cool completely before cutting and serving.

POWDERED BLUEBERRY DONUTS

Makes 6 donuts

When I lived on the Upper East Side of Manhattan, I walked to the gym to work out at 6:45 every morning. It was winter and hella cold, but the smell of the fresh donuts from the bakery I passed always made me feel toasty. One Monday morning, I walked to the gym not knowing that the gym was closed in observance of President's Day. When you have your own company, you tend not to notice these sorts of things. I entered the front door of the building and walked the one flight up the stairs to find that the gym door was locked. As I turned around to leave, the front door wouldn't budge and I realized I had locked myself inside the building. *Inside.* Three passersby, one doorman, two dogs, and one shimmying of a credit card in the door jamb later, I was finally free. You know what I thought about that entire time? These powdered blueberry donuts. With their tantalizing pops of fresh berries, these fluffy donuts were my "break me outta here" inspiration. A short jog later and I was home, savoring every bite of these luscious treats.

• ● •• ●

1 cup gluten-free flour
¼ teaspoon baking soda
½ teaspoon baking powder
    Pinch of salt
½ cup unsweetened almond milk
¼ cup granulated sugar
¼ cup unsweetened applesauce
1 tablespoon coconut oil, melted
2 teaspoons vanilla extract
½ cup fresh blueberries
¼ cup powdered sugar

note

Try replacing the blueberries with raspberries or even chocolate chips. Or hey, why not both?!

1 Preheat the oven to 325°F. Lightly spray a donut pan with nonstick cooking spray.

2 In a small bowl, whisk together the flour, baking soda, baking powder, and salt. In a medium bowl, mix together the almond milk, sugar, applesauce, coconut oil, and vanilla. Slowly add the flour mixture and stir until well blended and smooth. Gently stir in the blueberries until evenly dispersed.

3 Scoop the batter into the donut pan, filling ¾ of the way full. Bake until the donuts begin to lightly brown, 15 to 20 minutes. Remove from oven and let cool slightly in the pan before removing.

4 Once cool, gently dip the donuts in a small bowl of the powdered sugar or sift the powdered sugar over the top to coat evenly before serving.

BEIGNETS

Makes about 12 beignets

I tasted my first beignet at 4 a.m. at Café du Monde after partying for hours through the streets of New Orleans with a new friend after the NCAA basketball championships. Talk about a wild night! When the beads were all thrown and the parties began to wind down, my new friend and I found ourselves separated from the rest of our group, yet in the best place of all: standing in front of Café du Monde. Should we continue searching for our friends? Or stop and eat beignets? No-brainer. These vegan, gluten-free beignets aren't the same ones we devoured that night, but if you blow the powdered sugar in your friend's face as you enjoy these warm billowy darlings, I promise you'll get the same New Orleans effect.

¾ cup unsweetened almond milk

¾ cup warm water

2 tablespoons vegetable oil, plus more for frying

1 tablespoon granulated sugar

1½ teaspoons active dry yeast

½ teaspoon salt

3 cups gluten-free flour

½ cup powdered sugar, for dusting

note

✳ ✳ ✳ ✳ ✳ ✳ ✳ ✳ ✳ ✳ ✳ ✳ ✳

The more powdered sugar you pile on top, the more like New Orleans–style beignets these become.

1 In a large bowl, stir together the almond milk, water, vegetable oil, sugar, yeast, and salt. Let sit for 5 minutes.

2 Slowly beat in the flour until a thick dough forms. Cover the bowl and let the dough rise until doubled in size, 30 to 60 minutes.

3 Heat 2 inches of vegetable oil in a frying pan over medium-high heat. While the oil heats, roll the dough out on a floured surface until ¼-inch thick and cut into 2-inch squares with a pizza cutter. Alternatively, form the dough into tablespoon-size balls.

4 Working in batches, carefully drop the dough squares or balls into the hot oil, taking care not to crowd the pan. Fry until golden brown, flipping once, 3 to 4 minutes per batch. Transfer the beignets to a paper towel–lined plate to drain. Repeat with the remaining dough.

5 Sprinkle the beignets with powdered sugar and serve warm.

CHOCOLATE MOLTEN CUPCAKES

Makes 12 to 14 cupcakes

Do certain desserts remind you of certain people? They do for me. This chocolate cupcake exploding with warm melty chocolate reminds me of Alex. Alex loves dessert almost as much as I do. Almost. His favorite dessert? Molten chocolate cake from Chili's. When we were dating, we would go to Chili's sometimes just for dessert. No tacos. No quesadillas. Just molten chocolate cake. Who *does* that? I don't anymore, of course. Mainly because I've perfected this vegan version of that classic.

• •••••

1½ teaspoons distilled white vinegar
½ cup unsweetened almond milk
¾ cup gluten-free flour
¾ cup unsweetened cocoa powder
¾ cup granulated sugar
¾ teaspoon baking soda
½ teaspoon baking powder
¼ teaspoon salt
¼ cup unsweetened applesauce
¼ cup warm water
¾ teaspoon vanilla extract
½ cup chocolate chips
1 (12-ounce) jar Dollop Gourmet Hot Chocolate vegan frosting

> ### note
> If the lava level here is not up to your standards, double or triple the amount of chocolate chips you add to the middle of each cupcake and watch the chocolate flow.

1 Preheat the oven to 350°F. Spray a silicone cupcake mold with nonstick cooking spray.

2 Pour the vinegar into a ½ cup measure. Add enough almond milk to come to the brim. Let sit until slightly thickened, 5 to 10 minutes.

3 In a medium bowl, whisk together the flour, cocoa powder, sugar, baking soda, baking powder, and salt. Add the applesauce, water, vanilla, and the almond milk mixture and beat until batter is blended and smooth (it will be thin and runny).

4 Pour the batter into the prepared cupcake mold. Place 10 or so chocolate chips in the center of each cup of batter, pushing down gently so that some of them sink. Bake until the tops of the cupcakes spring back when you touch them, 16 to 18 minutes. Remove from the oven and let cool for 5 minutes before topping with the chocolate frosting. Serve at once.

VANILLA CUPCAKES

Makes 24 mini cupcakes

My top-selling frosting flavor? Vanilla. The most popular ice cream flavor? Vanilla. The number one rated cupcake flavor? Vanilla. As adventurous as we think our taste buds have become, vanilla still reigns supreme in this country. That's why I had to give you a standard yet incredibly delicious vegan gluten-free vanilla cupcake. If this plainness isn't your style, trust me, you'll be glad it's in your repertoire because it's bound to be a fave of someone close to you. Just you see!

● ˙ ●● ●

1½ teaspoons distilled white vinegar
½ cup unsweetened almond milk
1 cup plus 2 tablespoons gluten-free flour
½ teaspoon baking soda
¼ teaspoon baking powder
¼ teaspoon salt
½ cup granulated sugar
3 tablespoons safflower oil
1½ teaspoons vanilla extract
½ of a 12-ounce jar Dollop Gourmet Madagascar Vanilla vegan frosting

1 Preheat the oven to 350°F. Line a mini cupcake tin with liners.

2 Pour the vinegar into a ½ cup measure. Add enough almond milk to come to the brim. Let sit until slightly thickened, 5 to 10 minutes.

3 In a small bowl, whisk together the flour, baking soda, baking powder, and salt. In a medium bowl, mix together the sugar, safflower oil, and vanilla. Add the almond milk mixture and mix until just combined. Slowly add the flour mixture, beating until smooth.

4 Scoop the batter into the prepared tin. Bake until a toothpick inserted into the center comes out clean, 10 to 13 minutes. Remove from the oven and let cool before topping with the vanilla frosting.

NOTE

✳ ✳ ✳ ✳ ✳ ✳ ✳ ✳ ✳ ✳ ✳ ✳ ✳

Make sure not to overbeat or you will end up with rather dense cupcakes. If that's your style, whip it like there's no tomorrow. Go crazy with the toppings for these little guys! With a vanilla base and vanilla frosting, the toppings can really shine here. Try vegan sprinkles, fresh berries, vegan mini chocolate chips, or chopped pistachios. Try cutting a hole in the top of a cooled cupcake and adding a spoonful of vegan vanilla pudding, whipped cream, or Dollop Gourmet Sea Salted Caramel frosting before topping with frosting

SALTED CARAMEL PUMPKIN SPICE CUPCAKES

Makes 12 to 14 cupcakes

Salted caramel *and* pumpkin spice? Yeah, I know; this dessert is like a trend explosion. The subtle saltiness and buttery caramel pairs so well with pumpkin, I just couldn't resist matching them up. These cupcakes are moist, light, and oh so perfect for a fall day.

• • • •

1 cup gluten-free flour
¼ teaspoon baking soda
½ teaspoon baking powder
¼ teaspoon salt
¼ cup palm shortening
½ cup plus 1 tablespoon granulated sugar
½ cup canned pumpkin
¼ cup unsweetened applesauce
1 teaspoon pumpkin pie extract
1 (12-ounce) jar Dollop Gourmet Sea Salted Caramel vegan frosting
2 sheets vegan graham crackers, crushed
Ground cinnamon, for sprinkling

note
✳ ✳ ✳ ✳ ✳ ✳ ✳ ✳ ✳ ✳ ✳ ✳
Having a fall bash with lots of guests? You can turn any cupcake recipe into mini cupcakes. You'll generally get three minis for every one standard-size cupcake. Minis need less baking time—count on 6 to 8 minutes per batch.

1 Preheat the oven to 350°F. Line a cupcake tin with liners.

2 In a small bowl, whisk together the flour, baking soda, baking powder, and salt. In a medium bowl, cream the shortening until smooth. Add the sugar and continue mixing. Add the pumpkin, applesauce, and pumpkin pie extract and mix until blended. Slowly add the flour mixture and mix until well blended. Scrape down the sides of the bowl and continue mixing 1 minute more.

3 Scoop the batter into the lined tin and bake until a toothpick inserted in the center comes out with moist crumbs attached, 18 to 20 minutes. Remove from the oven and cool completely.

4 Frost the cooled cupcakes with caramel frosting. Sprinkle the tops with crushed graham crackers and ground cinnamon.

CARROT CAKE

Serves 6 to 8

If you're a carrot cake lover, you'll love this moist, classic treat. Spread some homemade vegan cream cheese frosting on top and you'll be licking your fingers as you eat.

1 cup gluten-free flour
1 teaspoon baking soda
¾ teaspoon ground cinnamon
⅛ teaspoon ground nutmeg
⅛ teaspoon ground ginger
Pinch of salt
1¼ cups shredded carrots
½ cup packed light brown sugar
¼ cup unsweetened applesauce
¼ cup vegetable oil
2 teaspoons vanilla extract

note

Try adding walnuts and currants or raisins. Frost with vegan cream cheese frosting or Dollop Gourmet Madagascar Vanilla frosting.

1 Preheat the oven to 350°F. Spray an 8-inch-square baking pan with nonstick cooking spray.

2 In a small bowl, whisk together the flour, baking soda, cinnamon, nutmeg, ginger, and salt. In a medium bowl, mix together the carrots, brown sugar, applesauce, oil, and vanilla. Add the flour mixture and mix until just blended, taking care not to overmix.

3 Pour evenly into the prepared baking pan and bake until a toothpick inserted in the center comes out dry, about 35 minutes. If frosting, let cool completely first.

RED WINE CHOCOLATE CAKE
WITH RASPBERRY FROSTING

Serves 6 to 8

Not many people know this about me, but I eat chocolate and drink a glass (or two) of red wine every night. Like the French, I understand the merits and health benefits of these two indulgences. Although I've read that red wine and dark chocolate are good for the body, I find they really benefit my sanity—they make me happy! And since we're all here on Earth to be happy, I'm going to enjoy my red wine and chocolate for as long as I can. Speaking of happiness, if you ever see me lounging in my PJs eating this moist and decadent red wine dark chocolate cake, you will find me in a state referred to as "pure bliss."

1 tablespoon apple cider vinegar

1 cup unsweetened almond milk

2 cups gluten-free flour

¾ cup dark unsweetened cocoa powder

2 teaspoons baking soda

¾ teaspoon salt

1¾ cups granulated sugar

1 cup vegetable oil

1 cup dark red wine

½ cup unsweetened applesauce

1 teaspoon vanilla extract

½ cup dark chocolate or semi-sweet chocolate chips

1 (12-ounce) jar Dollop Gourmet Madagascar Vanilla vegan frosting

1 cup fresh raspberries

1 Preheat the oven to 350°F. Spray a 9×13-inch cake pan with nonstick cooking spray.

2 Pour the vinegar into a 1-cup measuring cup. Add enough almond milk to come to the brim. Let sit until thickened, about 10 minutes.

3 In a medium bowl, whisk together the flour, cocoa powder, baking soda, and salt. In a separate bowl, mix together the sugar, vegetable oil, red wine, applesauce, vanilla, and almond milk mixture. Slowly add the flour mixture, mixing until blended. Add the chocolate chips and stir to combine.

4 Pour the batter into the prepared pan and bake until a toothpick inserted comes out with moist crumbs attached, 30 to 35 minutes. Remove from the oven and let cool completely.

5 In the bowl of a stand mixer, beat the frosting on medium speed. Slowly add the raspberries and beat until the desired consistency is reached. Spread the frosting over the cooled cake and serve.

note

Try making this cake even more chocolatey by using chocolate frosting instead of vanilla. Either way, it tastes even better the next day!

MIXED BERRY BANANA CAKE

Serves 6 to 8

Brimming with four different kinds of berries and sweet mashed bananas, this cake makes the perfect summer dessert. A warm muggy day, lounging on a blanket under the shade of an old oak tree, good book in hand, and a plate of this moist fruity cake—that's what I call heaven.

• ∙•∙ •

2 cups gluten-free flour

2 teaspoons baking powder

⅛ teaspoon salt

¾ cup granulated sugar

⅓ cup coconut oil

2 teaspoons vanilla extract

1⅔ cups mashed bananas

¼ cup unsweetened almond milk

¼ cup diced fresh strawberries

¼ cup fresh blueberries

¼ cup fresh raspberries

¼ cup fresh blackberries

¼–½ cup Dollop Gourmet Madagascar Vanilla vegan frosting

1 Preheat the oven to 350°F. Line a 9-inch-square baking pan or a round pan with parchment paper.

2 In a small bowl, whisk together the flour, baking powder, and salt. In a large bowl, beat together the sugar and coconut oil. Add the vanilla and mix until incorporated. Add the bananas and continue mixing until well combined. Add the flour mixture, alternating with the almond milk, and mix until just combined, taking care not to overmix. Gently fold the berries into the batter.

3 Spoon the batter into the prepared pan, smoothing the top with a spatula. Bake until a toothpick inserted in the center comes out with moist crumbs attached, 40 to 45 minutes. Remove from the oven and let cool completely.

4 Microwave the frosting at 30-second intervals until softened, stirring until smooth. Gently spread over the cake.

BREAD PUDDING WITH BOURBON SAUCE

Serves 6 to 8

Gosh, how I used to love bread pudding: warm, gooey bread tasting of cinnamon and vanilla and crowned with toasty, crusty tops . . . My mouth waters at the thought. But when I discovered I could no longer eat gluten or dairy, my dreams of bread pudding stayed just that—dreams. That is, until now. Feel free to double the recipe for the bourbon sauce if you like a little extra buzz.

BREAD PUDDING

2 tablespoons ground flax seeds

6 tablespoons water

2 cups unsweetened almond milk

¼ cup palm shortening

½ cup granulated sugar

¼ teaspoon ground nutmeg

1 teaspoon ground cinnamon

¼ teaspoon salt

1 teaspoon vanilla extract

6 cups soft vegan gluten-free bread, cut into 1-inch cubes

½ cup raisins

BOURBON SAUCE

¼ cup packed dark brown sugar

2 tablespoons bourbon

1 tablespoon coconut oil

1 teaspoon vanilla extract

Pinch of salt

> **note**
>
> Subbing regular bread for the gluten-free breads works just as well. Add a little crunch by tossing in some chopped walnuts and pecans.

1 Preheat the oven to 350°F. Spray a 9×13-inch baking pan with nonstick cooking spray.

2 To make the bread pudding, stir together the ground flax seeds and water in a bowl. Let sit until thickened, 10 to 15 minutes.

3 Heat the almond milk and shortening in a saucepan over medium heat, stirring constantly, until shortening is melted and milk is hot, taking care not to bring to a boil. Remove from heat.

4 Stir the sugar, nutmeg, cinnamon, salt, and vanilla into the flax mixture. Place the cubed bread in a large bowl. Pour the sugar mixture over the bread, tossing to coat as evenly as possible. Pour the milk mixture over the bread, tossing to coat evenly. Gently fold in the raisins. Let mixture sit for 15 to 20 minutes.

5 Spread the bread mixture evenly in the prepared baking pan and bake until the top begins to brown, 40 to 45 minutes.

6 While the bread pudding is baking, make the bourbon sauce. Combine the brown sugar, bourbon, coconut oil, vanilla, and salt in a small saucepan. Stirring constantly, bring to a boil over medium heat until slightly thickened. Remove from the heat and keep warm.

7 Pour the bourbon sauce over the warm bread pudding and serve at once.

> **note**
>
> Bread pudding doesn't store and reheat very well, so you'll want to share this one with friends right away. They'll love you for it.

PEANUT BUTTER AND JELLY BANANA BREAD

Serves 6 to 8

My mom never baked when I was growing up. My grandmother didn't bake, either. In fact, no one in my family baked. Where did *I* come from then, you're wondering? I wonder that myself! My mom's good friend, Shelly, made all the staples, each one better than the next. Moist and dense, with a sensation of semi-healthiness (not that I cared—I was a kid!), Shelly's banana and zucchini breads spread with a schmear of butter rocked my butterfly-print socks. Inspired by those school days, this banana bread takes things up a notch. Instead of butter, this dessert is brimming with creamy peanut butter goodness and bright strawberry jam—just like the sandwiches my mom used to make (she may not have baked, but she could make a mean PB&J!).

● ₒ●●

1 cup gluten-free flour
¾ teaspoon baking soda
¼ teaspoon salt
4 tablespoons palm shortening
¼ cup granulated sugar
¼ cup packed dark brown sugar
½ cup mashed ripe banana (1 large banana)
⅓ cup natural no-stir peanut butter
¼ cup unsweetened applesauce
½ teaspoon vanilla extract
2½ tablespoons strawberry jam, divided

note

Try different jam flavors! Grape, apricot, raspberry... there are so many ways to make this recipe your own. You can also try subbing chunky peanut butter, almond butter, or vegan chocolate hazelnut butter.

1 Preheat the oven to 325°F. Lightly spray a loaf pan with nonstick cooking spray.

2 In a small bowl, whisk together the flour, baking soda, and salt. In the bowl of a stand mixer, cream together the shortening and sugars. Add the mashed banana, peanut butter, applesauce, and vanilla and continue mixing. Slowly add the flour mixture and blend until smooth.

3 Spread half of the batter in the prepared pan. Drop 1½ tablespoons jam on top and swirl the jam through the batter with a knife, covering the surface evenly. Spread the remaining batter on top. Drop the remaining 1 tablespoon jam on top and swirl through the batter with a knife.

4 Bake until a toothpick inserted in the center comes out with moist crumbs attached, 60 to 70 minutes. Let cool before serving.

PEPPERMINT MOCHA BROWNIE BATTER DIP

Serves 6 to 8

This is going to make me sound a little crazy, but I'm going to share it anyway. You see, this recipe was supposed to be for brownies, but the batter didn't make it into the oven. Because *I ate it*. I know, I know, you're not supposed to eat the brownie batter. But I promise this one is safe to eat. It's not only safe, it's rich, dark, minty, and oh so tantalizing. Actually, that doesn't sound safe at all! Now go—get your brownie danger on.

• •• •

2 tablespoons ground flax seeds
7 tablespoons water, divided
2 tablespoons instant coffee
¾ cup granulated sugar
½ cup packed dark brown sugar
½ cup coconut oil, melted
1 teaspoon vanilla extract
½ cup unsweetened cocoa powder
½ cup unsweetened dark cocoa powder
½ cup crushed candy canes
   Vegan graham crackers, for dipping

1 In a small bowl, mix the ground flax seeds with 6 tablespoons of the water and let sit until thickened, 5 to 10 minutes. In a separate small bowl, mix the instant coffee with the remaining 1 tablespoon of water until fully dissolved.

2 In a medium bowl, mix together the sugars and coconut oil until well combined. Add the vanilla and flax seed and coffee mixtures and mix well. Add both cocoa powders and mix until well combined and smooth. Scoop the mixture into a serving bowl and sprinkle with the crushed candy canes. Serve with graham crackers for dipping.

note
Are you like me and not into the caffeine rush? Don't fret, you can use decaf coffee for this one. Try serving with vanilla wafer cookies or vegan marshmallows on a skewer.

CHOCOLATE PRETZEL TOFFEE

Serves 6 to 8

My pup, Donald, and I arrived in Boulder with a day to spare before I had to be at the news station in Denver to talk about Thanksgiving desserts. I said to Donald, "Hey bud, let's go for a little walk toward the mountains over there." Three hours later, we had managed to climb a giant treacherous peak. Between the high altitude, the lack of water, the fact that I hadn't eaten breakfast (since we were just going for a *short* walk), and the massive boulders I scaled while carrying a 25-pound dog, I didn't think I'd make it back down. And I desperately wished I had packed a snack. Specifically, a snack like this yummy, crunchy, sweet, and salty chocolate pretzel toffee. We eventually made it down the mountain intact, with lasting memories and a great story to share, as well as an instant hankering for chocolate pretzel toffee whenever I think of Colorado.

• • • • •

8 ounces gluten-free vegan pretzel twists, coarsely broken
1 cup plus 2 tablespoons vegetable margarine, divided
1 cup packed light brown sugar
2¼ cups chocolate chips
½ teaspoon Himalayan sea salt

note

Try subbing vegan crackers for the pretzels. You'll get addicted, I know it!

1 Preheat the oven to 375°F. Line a baking sheet with parchment paper. Spread the broken pretzels evenly on the baking sheet.

2 In a small saucepan over medium heat, add 1 cup of the margarine and the brown sugar, stirring until the margarine melts and the mixture starts to simmer. Cook, without stirring, for 3 to 4 minutes. Pour the mixture over the pretzels, coating them evenly. Bake the pretzels for 5 minutes.

3 Microwave the chocolate chips with the remaining 2 tablespoons of margarine in a small bowl at 30-second intervals until melted and smooth.

4 Spread the chocolate mixture evenly over the pretzels in a thin layer. Sprinkle with the salt. Let cool completely before breaking into pieces and serving.

2 *Very Easy* VEGAN DESSERTS

This is a fantastic time to be vegan! While launching Dollop Gourmet vegan products, I've realized how many other incredible companies are also developing vegan products of their own right now. As an exhibitor, I've had the pleasure of scouring the natural product trade shows, and now I'm bringing you the inside scoop on the best baking products to add to your vegan cupboard. From raw ingredients, such as sugar minus the bone char, to finished products, such as cookies and marshmallows, there are so many tasty vegan products out there that making semi-homemade desserts today is a breeze—a very easy breeze. Throughout this chapter, I'll introduce you to some of my favorite vegan products that you can find in your local grocery store or online and show you what delicious treats you can make with them.

BLUEBERRY LEMON CHEESECAKE

Serves 6 to 8

Every guy I date loves cheesecake. This gets annoying because I can't eat cheesecake. How can we split dessert if you order what I can't eat? Oh, shoot, I guess I'll have to get my own dessert then. But sometimes it's sweet to take two forks to one dessert . . . there's an intimacy there. So if you catch yourself in the same predicament, there's only one thing to do: create a deliciously decadent vegan cheesecake that is the spitting image of the dairy-laden dessert. This blueberry lemon cheesecake is so creamy good I bet your guy won't even notice the difference.

2 (8-ounce) packages vegan cream cheese

1 cup granulated sugar

2 tablespoons fresh lemon juice
Pinch of salt

2 cups fresh blueberries, divided

1 prepared vegan gluten-free graham cracker crust

> ### note
> ✳ ✳ ✳ ✳ ✳ ✳ ✳ ✳ ✳ ✳ ✳
> You can make your own graham cracker crust by combining crushed graham crackers with melted vegan butter and pressing the mixture into the bottom of a pie pan. Bake at 350°F until golden, 15 to 20 minutes. Let cool before filling with the cheesecake mixture. Both Daiya and Kite Hill Creamery make excellent vegan cream cheese.

1 Preheat the oven to 350°F.

2 In a medium bowl, mix together the cream cheese, sugar, lemon juice, and salt until smooth. Pour ½ cup of the blueberries over the bottom of the graham cracker crust. Spread the cream cheese mixture on top so that it evenly covers the blueberries.

3 Bake until golden brown, about 35 minutes. Remove from the oven and let cool slightly before refrigerating until cold, at least 1 hour.

4 Scatter the remaining blueberries over the top of the cheesecake and serve immediately.

BOSTON CREAM CAKE

I have a friend named Steve who is mostly annoying, but he also knows how to be a good friend. Sometimes. He's a comedian, so he always thinks he's funny. I usually think I'm funnier. Anyway, I swear he's asked me about ten times for a Boston cream pie recipe. I'm not sure why it's his favorite dessert or why he never saves recipes, but whenever I think of Boston cream, I now think of Steve. Maybe that was his plan—to always be in my head. Dammit, Steve, that's just like you! This Boston Cream Cake is a variation of the traditional pie, and I think it's even better. With its thick custard filling and super moist crumb, this chocolate-frosted delight is worth every annoying thought of Steve it inspired.

2 tablespoons ground flax seeds

6 tablespoons water

1 (15- to 17-ounce) box vegan gluten-free vanilla cake mix

¼ cup unsweetened applesauce

1 (3.9-ounce) packet instant vanilla pudding

1 cup unsweetened vanilla almond milk

1 (12-ounce) jar Dollop Gourmet Hot Chocolate vegan frosting

note

When using a cake mix, I generally substitute unsweetened almond milk if regular milk is called for. I like to use Jell-O® Simply Good Vanilla Bean pudding mix. Use two packets of pudding and double the amount of vanilla almond milk for an extra gooey pudding cake.

1 Preheat the oven to 350°F. Spray a 9×13-inch cake pan with nonstick cooking spray.

2 In a small bowl, mix together the flax seeds and water. Let sit until thickened, about 10 minutes.

3 Prepare the cake mix according to the directions on the box, substituting the applesauce and flax seed mixture for the eggs. Spread the batter in the prepared pan and bake until a toothpick inserted in the center comes out with moist crumbs attached, 30 to 35 minutes. Remove from the oven and let cool slightly.

4 When the cake is relatively cool, use the handle of a wooden spoon or a wooden skewer to poke holes about ½ inch apart over the top of the cake. In a medium bowl, mix together the pudding packet and almond milk until well blended. Before it begins to thicken, pour the mixture over the cake, spreading it in an even layer. Refrigerate the cake for 1 hour.

5 Microwave the opened jar of frosting at 15-second intervals until smooth and easy to spread. Pour over top of cake and spread evenly.

BANANA COCONUT CREAM PIE

Serves 6 to 8

Need to whip up a pie quickly for a holiday function? I've got you covered this year. Look no farther than this sure-to-please spin on classic banana cream pie. Coconut is all the rage these days, so you've got those trendsetters taken care of. Toss in some bananas and creamy vanilla pudding, and this vegan gluten-free pie will have everyone at the office shindig singing your praises.

3 ripe bananas, sliced, divided

1 prepared vegan gluten-free graham cracker crust

2 (3.9-ounce) packets instant vanilla pudding mix

1 cup unsweetened almond milk

1 (9-ounce) tub coconut whipped cream

NOTE

Try sprinkling the pie with toasted shredded coconut for an extra coconutty crunch.

1 Arrange one-third of the banana slices over the bottom of the graham cracker crust.

2 Pour the instant pudding mixes into a medium bowl. Slowly add the almond milk, whisking until smooth.

3 Pour the pudding over the bananas in the crust, smoothing the top. Top with another one-third of the sliced bananas. Chill the pie until firm, about 1 hour.

4 Spread the whipped cream over the chilled pie. Decorate with the remaining banana slices. Serve chilled.

TIRAMISU **TRIFLE**

Serves 6 to 8

The last time I had caffeine, my heart began to race, my hands began to shake, and my mind felt like it had suddenly become a tornado about to take down the nearest town. And that, my friends, is why I no longer drink caffeine—no one wants my mind taking down their town. Trust me. But there I was, having cut out caffeine, dairy, and gluten, all the ingredients of tiramisu. The thought of never savoring creamy espresso-soaked cake again just about made me cry. Which is why I created this vegan gluten-free *decaf* bundle of tiramisu joy. I kid you not, I ate three of these trifles in one sitting the first time I made this recipe.

● ₂●●

1 (15- to 17-ounce) box vegan gluten-free vanilla cake mix

¼ to ½ cup unsweetened applesauce

¼ cup plus 1 tablespoon instant decaf coffee powder, divided

1 cup cold water

4 ounces vegan cream cheese

3¼ cups powdered sugar

4 tablespoons coffee-flavored liqueur, such as Kahlúa®

½ cup nondairy whipped cream

2 tablespoons unsweetened cocoa powder

note
✳ ✳ ✳ ✳ ✳ ✳ ✳ ✳ ✳ ✳
There are plenty of vanilla cake mixes out there. My favorite gluten-free one for this recipe is Pamela's. For the whipped cream, I recommend So Delicious CocoWhip™, while Kite Hill Creamery and Daiya both make great vegan cream cheeses.

1 Make the cake following the directions on the box, using ¼ cup applesauce in place of each egg (up to 2 eggs total). Bake the cake and let it cool. Once cool, break the cake apart with your hands or cut into 1-inch cubes.

2 In a small bowl, stir ¼ cup of the instant coffee powder into the water until fully dissolved.

3 In a medium bowl, whip the cream cheese. Add the powdered sugar and continue mixing, scraping down sides of the bowl as needed. Add the liqueur and the remaining 1 tablespoon of instant coffee powder and continue mixing. Gently fold in the nondairy whipped cream.

4 You can make 1 large trifle using a large trifle dish or mini trifles using individual dishes. To assemble, cover the bottom of the trifle dish with some of the cake pieces. Drizzle some of the coffee over the cake, then top with a layer of the cream cheese mixture. Repeat layering with the remaining ingredients until you reach the top of the dish. Sprinkle the top with cocoa powder. Refrigerate before serving for best flavor or serve immediately if you simply can't wait!

DOUBLE CHOCOLATE CRISPY RICE DONUTS

Makes 6 to 8 donuts

Seriously friends, I'm not even sure what more to say about this recipe than what the title describes. (Oh, yeah, there are sprinkles, too!) You should call me Santa for this one. Merry treating, my loves.

3 tablespoons palm shortening
1 (10-ounce) bag mini marshmallows
¼ cup chocolate chips
4 cups vegan gluten-free crisped rice cereal
½ cup Dollop Gourmet Hot Chocolate vegan frosting
Sprinkles

note

If you don't have a donut pan, you can make these in traditional squares by pressing the mixture into a parchment-lined baking pan. For the crisped rice cereal, I used Nature's Path Envirokidz Organic Koala Crisp Cereal. I recommend My Dandies brand for the marshmallows. For the frosting, Dollop Gourmet Hot Chocolate, of course.

1 Lightly spray a donut pan with nonstick cooking spray.

2 Melt the shortening in a saucepan over medium-low heat. Add the marshmallows and cook, stirring constantly, until melted. Add the chocolate chips and stir until melted. Add the rice cereal and stir until evenly coated.

3 Press the cereal mixture evenly into each cavity of the donut pan, working quickly before it cools. Refrigerate until completely cool.

4 Remove the "donuts" from the pan and frost with chocolate frosting. Decorate with sprinkles.

WEDDING CAKE DONUTS

Makes about 8 donuts

We catered a lot of weddings at my bakery. Some days my bakery was stacked floor to ceiling with boxes of wedding cupcakes ready to be picked up or delivered. One breezy summer day we had so many weddings scheduled that we ran out of counter space. Because I'm always a thinker, I decided to stack the boxes on the windowsill. Because I'm not always a think-it-through-er, I didn't think to close the window first. You can probably guess what happened next.... While the whole staff was busy frosting cupcakes in the kitchen, we heard the loudest, most ominous *CRASH!* come from the front room. Running in, I saw boxes upon boxes of toppled cupcakes decorating the floor. Donuts, like these wedding cake donuts, would have been a hell of a lot easier to clean up. With their hint of almond and Champagne essence, these are the perfect vegan treat to celebrate a special day! Or even just a day without a floor full of fallen cupcakes.

● ● ● ●

1 (15- to 17-ounce) box vegan gluten-free vanilla cake mix

¼ to ½ cup unsweetened applesauce

½ teaspoon almond extract

1 (12-ounce) jar Dollop Gourmet Madagascar Vanilla vegan frosting

2 tablespoons dry Champagne

2 teaspoons gold sanding sugar for decorating (optional)

note

These also make a fabulous New Year's Eve dessert to "ring" in the new year! If you want to make them even more special, try using strawberry Champagne. It was a huge hit at my bakery.

1 Preheat the oven according to the directions on the cake mix box. Spray a donut pan with nonstick cooking spray.

2 Make the cake mix following the directions on the box, using ¼ cup applesauce in place of each egg (up to 2 eggs total). Stir in the almond extract.

3 Pour the batter into the prepared donut pan (you may have to bake in batches if your pan isn't big enough). Bake until the donuts begin to turn golden, 20 to 25 minutes. Remove from the oven and let cool.

4 In a medium bowl, beat the frosting with the Champagne until soft and fluffy. Frost the tops of the cooled donuts and sprinkle with the sanding sugar, if desired.

PINEAPPLE UPSIDE-DOWN DONUTS

Makes 6 to 8 donuts

The day I made the leap and picked up Donald from the shelter (without even thinking to bring a collar or a leash), my life was turned upside down. Though I had a dog growing up, it was mostly my dad who took care of Magpie. I truly didn't know what to do. Donald stared at me. I stared at him. But eventually we figured each other out, and now Donald is my furry best friend who always tries to steal my food, especially when it's fruit. But I wouldn't have it any other way. Inspired by Donald's love for fruit and my love for donuts (okay, Donald loves donuts too, obviously), I bring you these sprightly, topsy-turvy pineapple donuts. If you don't have a rescue dog, these delicious treats will turn your life upside down in the best way possible instead.

• •••

1 (15- to 17-ounce) box vegan gluten-free vanilla cake mix
¼ to ½ cup unsweetened applesauce
12 maraschino cherries, sliced
6 to 8 canned pineapple slices, drained

NOTE

If you don't have a donut pan you can make these in a cupcake pan. You can also use chopped pineapples instead of rings.

1 Preheat the oven according to the directions on the cake mix box. Spray a donut pan with nonstick cooking spray.

2 Make the cake mix following the directions on the box, using ¼ cup applesauce in place of each egg (up to 2 eggs total). Fold the cherries into the batter.

3 Place 1 pineapple slice in the bottom of each donut ring (you may have to bake in batches if your pan isn't big enough). Pour cake batter over the pineapple, filling three-quarters of the way. Bake until a toothpick inserted in the center comes out with moist crumbs attached, 25 to 30 minutes. Remove from oven and let cool in the pan.

COFFEE CAKE CORNBREAD

Serves 6 to 8

Three weeks after moving to L.A., I decided to get my car detailed (a dog + a month-long cross-country road trip = one messy car). That same day, I had the idea of making a cornbread-based coffeecake. So I searched Yelp for a car detailing place that was close to a grocery store. Can you believe I found one inside a parking garage beneath a Trader Joe's? Los Angeles rocks! I spent three hours wandering around Trader Joe's, waiting for my car and craving this moist, cinnamon-sweet coffeecake cornbread, but boy I'll tell you, it was *well* worth the wait.

FOR THE CRUMBLE

⅓ cup packed light brown sugar
½ teaspoon ground cinnamon
¼ teaspoon salt
4 tablespoons palm shortening, melted
½ cup gluten-free flour

FOR THE CAKE

¾ cup unsweetened almond milk
½ cup sunflower oil
⅓ cup unsweetened applesauce
1 (15-ounce) box gluten-free cornbread mix

> **note**
> ✳ ✳ ✳ ✳ ✳ ✳ ✳ ✳ ✳ ✳ ✳ ✳ ✳
> Trader Joe's gluten-free cornbread mix is spot-on for this recipe. *Mmmmm, I'm craving it now.*

1 Preheat the oven to 375°F. Spray an 8-inch-square cake pan with nonstick cooking spray.

2 To make the crumble, mix together the brown sugar, cinnamon, and salt in a small bowl. Stir in the melted shortening. Add the flour and mix until a crumbly mixture forms. Refrigerate while you make the cake mixture.

3 To make the cake, mix together the almond milk, sunflower oil, and applesauce in a medium bowl. Slowly add the cornbread mix and continue mixing for 2 to 3 minutes. Spread the mixture in the prepared pan. Sprinkle the crumble mixture on top. Let sit for 10 minutes before placing in the oven.

4 Bake until a toothpick inserted in the center comes out with moist crumbs attached, 20 to 25 minutes. Let cool before serving.

CHOCOLATE PEANUT BUTTER CAKE BITES

Makes about 12

When I was on *Cupcake Wars*, one of my cupcake creations was a chocolate cake with creamy peanut butter frosting. Sprinkles founder and judge Candace Nelson adored it, proclaiming it just like the ones sold at her shop. Quite the rave review, I'd say! Even though these chocolaty cake bites aren't made completely from scratch, they are quick and easy and have my stamp of approval for a winning combination that you too will adore.

• •••

1 (15- to 17-ounce) box vegan gluten-free chocolate cake mix
¼ to ½ cup unsweetened applesauce
1 (12-ounce) jar Dollop Gourmet Peanut Butter Cookie Dough vegan frosting
¼ cup chopped unsalted peanuts
Chocolate shavings

note
If you'd rather make full-size cupcakes because you're just *that* hungry, this recipe will make about 12 cupcakes. You may need to bake them an additional 5 to 10 minutes.

1 Preheat the oven according to the directions on the cake mix box. Spray two 9×13-inch rectangular pans with nonstick cooking spray.

2 Make the cake mix following the directions on the box, using ¼ cup applesauce in place of each egg (up to 2 eggs total). Divide the batter evenly between the two pans (the layers will be thin). Bake until a toothpick inserted in the center comes out clean, 15 to 20 minutes. Remove the cakes from the oven and let cool completely.

3 Once cool, cut 24 rounds from the cakes with a small circular cake cutter (12 rounds—or however many you get from the cutter you use—from each cake). Remove the cake circles from the pan. (Nibble on the cake scraps as your late-afternoon snack!)

4 Place the peanut butter frosting in a pastry bag fitted with a star tip. Pipe a small star of frosting on top of a cake round and place another cake round on top. Pipe a star of frosting on top of the second cake round and sprinkle the top with chopped peanuts and chocolate shavings. Repeat with the remaining cake rounds and frosting.

STRAWBERRY SHORTCAKE CUPS

Makes 12 to 14 cups

Remember that little doll dressed in a pink and white dress with strawberries all over it? She even smelled like strawberries. Well, I played with my beloved Strawberry Shortcake doll often when I was a child—so often that, to this day, if someone mentions strawberry shortcake, I think of that doll rather than the delicious summery dessert stuffed with fresh strawberries and fluffy cream. These tasty, bite-size versions of that classic dessert are the perfect size to share with a pint-size friend or doll, if you wish.

½ cup plus 2 tablespoons palm shortening, melted

3 tablespoons packed light brown sugar

6 sheets vegan graham crackers, crushed

1 (15- to 17-ounce) box vegan, gluten-free vanilla cake mix

¼ to ½ cup unsweetened applesauce

1 (7-ounce) can nondairy whipped cream

2 cups sliced fresh strawberries

note
In order to keep your shortcakes intact, take the time to cool them completely. But they'll taste just as good if your patience wears thin and you dig in while warm. (And, frankly, I wouldn't blame you if you can't wait!)

1 Preheat the oven according to the directions on the boxed cake mix. Line a cupcake pan with liners.

2 In a small bowl, stir together the melted shortening, brown sugar, and crushed graham crackers until a crust-like mixture forms. Firmly press 2 tablespoons of the mixture into the bottom of each cupcake liner. Refrigerate while you make the cake batter.

3 Make the cake mix following the directions on the box, using ¼ cup applesauce in place of each egg (up to 2 eggs total). Scoop the batter into the liners over the graham cracker crusts. Bake until a toothpick inserted in the center comes out clean, 15 to 20 minutes. Let cool completely.

4 Top each cake with whipped cream and sliced strawberries and serve at once.

BOURBON PEACH
COBBLER

Serves 10 to 12

I lived in Charlotte, North Carolina, for almost six months. I had moved there for a sales job that did not go well. The company sold stuff door-to-door—$5 coloring books, $10 knife sets, $20 pieces of luggage . . . let's just say it wasn't the brightest time of my life. At the end of the day, you could often find me sitting in my car full of unsold stuff, consoling myself with Bojangles cornbread and peach cobbler. Too bad that cobbler didn't have bourbon in it like this delectably easy recipe does. A bite of this warm and toasty bourbon-kissed peach cobbler will surely warm your spirits.

3 (15-ounce) cans peach halves in syrup, divided

4 tablespoons spiced bourbon

1 (15- to 17-ounce) box vegan gluten-free vanilla cake mix

½ cup vegan butter, melted

2 teaspoons ground cinnamon

Vegan ice cream, for serving

note

Try serving this cobbler with vegan whipped cream and a shot of bourbon to warm your soul.

1 Preheat the oven to 350°F. Spray a 9×13-inch baking pan with nonstick cooking spray.

2 Drain two of the cans of peaches and arrange the peaches in the dish. Add the remaining can of peaches, including its liquid, to the baking dish. Add the bourbon and stir gently to combine.

3 Sprinkle the dry cake mix evenly over the peaches to cover. Drizzle the melted vegan butter evenly over the top. Sprinkle with the cinnamon.

4 Bake until the top is golden, 50 minutes to 1 hour. Remove from the oven and serve warm with vegan ice cream.

BLUEBERRY CRANBERRY PINEAPPLE CRISP

Serves 10 to 12

Have you heard of the Magic Castle in Los Angeles? This exclusive, invite-only club is incredibly special. Inside, it's like something out of a Harry Potter film: the stools move, the owls speak, the piano plays any song you want all on its own. One evening, I found myself onstage at the Magic Castle performing a magic trick in front of a crowd, opening a show for a real magician. What a night! And now, with my newfound magician skills I present you with this fabulous blueberry cranberry pineapple crisp recipe that magically comes together in the blink of an eye. Poof! Before you know it, you'll be digging into a hot, buttery bowl of fruit crisp topped with cold vanilla ice cream. Abracadabra!

3 cups fresh blueberries

1 cup chopped fresh pineapple

½ cup fresh cranberries

3 tablespoons granulated sugar

1 tablespoon cornstarch

1 teaspoon vanilla extract

1 cup vegan gluten-free graham crackers, crushed

6 tablespoons vegan butter, softened and cut into cubes

Vegan ice cream, for serving

1 Preheat the oven to 375°F. Lightly spray a 2-quart baking dish with nonstick cooking spray.

2 In a large bowl, gently stir together the blueberries, pineapple, cranberries, sugar, cornstarch, and vanilla. Pour into the prepared baking dish.

3 Combine the graham crackers with the vegan butter, mixing with a fork until coarse, moist crumbs form. Sprinkle the crumbs over the fruit.

4 Bake until the top is golden brown and fruit is bubbling, 30 to 35 minutes. Serve warm with vegan ice cream.

note
✳ ✳ ✳ ✳ ✳ ✳ ✳ ✳ ✳ ✳ ✳
You can use crushed vegan sugar cookies if you can't find graham crackers.

SWEET POTATO CRISP

Serves 10 to 12

I love sweet potatoes so much that I made a sweet potato cupcake when I competed on *Cupcake Wars*. They loved it, and I won. End of story.

Okay fine, I'll continue the story. The cupcake was stuffed with a blueberry ketchup and topped with brown sugar frosting and it was maddeningly delicious! You can find the recipe in my first book, *The Dollop Book of Frosting*. I couldn't complete *this* book without a sweet potato dessert recipe. Enter this super easy one-pan sweet potato crisp—it's downright heavenly.

● ● ● ●

1 (40-ounce) can sweet potatoes, drained
1 cup quick-cooking oats
1 cup packed light brown sugar
½ cup pecans, chopped
1½ teaspoons ground cinnamon
    Pinch of salt
½ cup refined coconut oil, melted
1 teaspoon vanilla extract

1 Preheat the oven to 400°F. Lightly spray an 8-inch-square baking pan with nonstick cooking spray.

2 Place the sweet potatoes in the prepared pan. In a medium bowl, mix together the oats, brown sugar, pecans, cinnamon, salt, melted coconut oil and vanilla. Spread the mixture evenly over the sweet potatoes.

3 Bake until the top begins to brown, 25 to 30 minutes. Serve warm.

MY OATMEAL CRÈME PIES

Makes 8 to 10 pies

Did you grow up eating Little Debbie snack cakes like I did? Just about every day when I was a kid, I found a sweet snack cake tucked in my lunch box. One of my favorites was the Oatmeal Cream Pie. Our high school cafeteria sold these cellophane-wrapped soft oatmeal cookies sandwiched with creamy vanilla frosting, and my friends and I went wild for them. Since I can't eat commercial snack cakes anymore, I've made it my mission to create and share better-for-you snack cakes with the world again. And what better snack cake to start with than the oatmeal crème pie? One bite and fond childhood memories will come flooding back.

1 tablespoon ground flax seeds

3 tablespoons water

2 cups rolled oats

1 cup gluten-free flour

1½ teaspoons ground cinnamon

½ teaspoon baking soda

¼ teaspoon salt

¾ cup vegan butter, chilled

¾ cup packed light brown sugar

2 teaspoons vanilla extract

1 (12-ounce) jar Dollop Gourmet Madagascar Vanilla vegan frosting

> ### note
>
> Try adding a couple teaspoons of cinnamon to the vanilla frosting to take your oatmeal crème pie up a spice notch. I like to use Bob's Red Mill Gluten-Free Oats and 1-to-1 Flour.

1 Preheat the oven to 350°F. Line a baking sheet with parchment paper.

2 In a small bowl, stir together the ground flax seeds and the water. Let sit until thickened, about 10 minutes.

3 In a large bowl, whisk together the oats, flour, cinnamon, baking soda, and salt. In a separate large bowl, cream together the vegan butter and sugar. Add the flax seed mixture and vanilla and mix for 1 minute more. Add the oat mixture and mix until all ingredients are incorporated and a thick dough forms. If the mixture is too dry, add water, 1 tablespoon at a time, until the dough holds together.

4 Roll tablespoon-size balls of dough and place on the baking sheet. Bake until the bottoms begin to turn golden, 15 to 18 minutes. Remove from the oven and let cool for a few minutes before removing from the baking sheet.

5 Once the cookies are completely cool, spread 1 to 2 tablespoons of vanilla frosting on the bottom of one cookie and sandwich with a second cookie. Repeat with the remaining cookies and frosting.

LEMON CAKE COOKIES

Makes 10 to 12 cookies

I've received a lot of hate mail in my day. How could anyone hate me, you're thinking? I'm not sure either. Anyway . . . My favorite was the time a girl posted a comment in all capitals on one of my YouTube videos calling me the "Cupcake Ke$ha." A real gem of a post! Some people can be so sour. And others are just downright sweet (I get love letters, too). Kind of like these easy, cakey lemon cookies where sweet and sour team up to give you one awesome *pow!* in the face. In the best way possible, of course.

2 tablespoons ground flax seeds

6 tablespoons water

1 (15- to 17-ounce) box vegan gluten-free vanilla cake mix

⅓ cup vegetable oil

1 tablespoon lemon extract

⅓ cup powdered sugar

1 In a small bowl, stir together the ground flax seeds and water. Let sit until thickened, 5 to 10 minutes.

2 In a medium bowl, mix together the cake mix, oil, lemon extract, and flax seed mixture until well blended. Chill the dough, covered, for 15 to 20 minutes.

3 Preheat the oven to 350°F. Line a baking sheet with parchment paper.

4 Place the powdered sugar in a small bowl. Drop teaspoon-size balls of dough in the sugar and toss gently until lightly coated. Arrange the balls on the baking sheet and flatten slightly.

5 Bake until the edges begin to turn golden, 8 to 11 minutes. Let cool before removing from the baking sheet.

RASPBERRY-FILLED CHOCOLATE COOKIES

Makes about 16 cookies

On December 1, 2016, after a month on the road doing a fabulous twelve-city media tour, Donald and I finally landed in our new home of Los Angeles! It was very exciting, to say the least. We were ready to embark on our new life of sun, fun, and glamour. I quickly secured a lovely new apartment and fully outfitted it with new furnishings. However, not more than two weeks later, I received a call from the top food accelerator program in the world, inviting me to move back to New York City to work for the next three months—a can't-miss opportunity. So what did I do? Packed a couple suitcases, grabbed Donald, and hopped on a direct flight to begin a new life back in Manhattan! Sometimes all you can do is laugh about life's timing. There wasn't much room in my tiny studio sublet on the Upper East Side to make elaborate desserts, which is how I came up with this two-ingredient, melt-in-your mouth cookie recipe. From L.A. to NYC, these little sweet joys will bring you timely pleasure wherever you are.

• • • •

1 (16-ounce) tub vegan chocolate cookie dough

ABOUT 1 cup raspberry jam

note
✳ ✳ ✳ ✳ ✳ ✳ ✳ ✳ ✳ ✳ ✳
There are a few vegan cookie dough brands out there, but my all-time favorite is Alpendough. Based in Colorado, this family-run company makes out-of-this-world chocolate cookie dough with a hint of almond. Don't worry, they ship. And you won't be disappointed.

1 Preheat the oven according to the directions on the cookie dough tub. Line two baking sheets with parchment paper.

2 Roll tablespoon-size balls of softened cookie dough in the palms of your hands. Press your thumb in the center of each ball to create an indentation. Drop ½ tablespoon raspberry jam into the indentation and wrap the cookie dough around the jam until it's fully covered. Place each filled ball on the baking sheets and press down gently. Repeat with the remaining cookie dough and jam.

3 Bake until cookies are just set, 8 to 10 minutes. Remove from the oven and let cool.

KEY LIME TRUFFLES

Makes about 24 truffles

My mom and I used to go to southwestern Florida every winter to visit her best friend, Mary. We'd shop, laze at Siesta Key beach, and dine al fresco in Boca Raton. Florida always makes me think of Key lime pie. Not once did we actually eat Key lime pie on those vacations, but small detail. What matters is that we were soaking up the Florida sunshine and enjoying life to its fullest! These citrusy truffles are like little balls of Florida sunshine. Make these real fast, then kick back, relax, and pretend you're soaking up some of those southern Florida rays.

● ● ●●

1 (15- to 17-ounce) box vegan gluten-free vanilla cake mix

¼ cup granulated sugar

7 tablespoons vegan butter, melted

1 teaspoon freshly grated lime zest

2 tablespoons fresh lime juice, preferably from Key limes

½ cup vegan gluten-free graham crackers, crushed

1 In a medium bowl, combine the cake mix, sugar, melted vegan butter, lime zest, and juice, stirring until the dough sticks together. Using your hands, roll the dough into smooth, tablespoon-size balls.

2 Place the crushed graham crackers in a small bowl. Roll the balls in the crushed graham crackers to coat.

3 Place the coated truffles in the freezer for 30 minutes to set.

note

To crush the graham crackers, place them in a sealed plastic bag and pound with a rolling pin until fine crumbs form. Get your aggression out here!

RUM BALLS

Makes 12 to 14 balls

I've never been a rum fan. Red wine, bourbon, or Scotch—now that's my jam. The only way to tempt me with rum is by pouring it into these tasty, nutty balls of fun. The spiced rum soaks into the sweet cookies and coconut like it's meant to be there, and the nuts add that toasty *je ne sais quoi*. *Mmm*, rum balls, you sure are my friends.

1 cup crushed vegan vanilla wafers or crunchy chocolate cookies

2 cups powdered sugar, divided

¾ cup finely chopped walnuts

½ cup unsweetened shredded coconut

2 tablespoons unsweetened cocoa powder (if using vanilla cookies)

Pinch of salt

3 tablespoons dark spiced rum

1 tablespoon maple syrup

1 In a medium bowl, mix together the crushed cookies, 1 cup of the powdered sugar, walnuts, coconut, cocoa powder (if using), and salt. Add the rum and maple syrup, and mix until the dough begins to stick together.

2 Chill the dough, covered, for 1 hour.

3 Place the remaining 1 cup powdered sugar in a small bowl. With your hands, roll the chilled dough into tablespoon-size balls, then roll in the powdered sugar until lightly coated. Chill until ready to serve.

CAKE BATTER BLONDIES

Makes 9 to 12 blondies

My mom is super into birthdays. I love this about her. Every year she makes sure she's the first person to call and wish me a happy birthday. We go out to dinner to whatever restaurant I choose, and she spends a lot of time picking out just the right cake with which to surprise me. She's never baked me a homemade cake, which is perfectly fine with me. There are so many excellent bakeries out there! But if I did ask for homemade cake, it might be in the form of these sprinkle-filled blondies. Wait—I take that back. These delightful blondies would be my midday birthday treat, with a ginormous decadent cake to follow in the evening. You can never have too much cake on your birthday!

• •••

1 (15- to 17-ounce) box vegan gluten-free vanilla cake mix

¼ cup safflower oil or melted refined coconut oil

3 tablespoons aquafaba

¼ cup unsweetened almond milk

4 tablespoons rainbow sprinkles

note

Make sure to pick colored sprinkles without confectioner's glaze. Confectioner's glaze isn't vegan and thus doesn't belong in these party blondies. If you don't want to use aquafaba, you can substitute unsweetened applesauce, which will produce blondies that are softer and a bit fluffier.

1 Preheat the oven to 350°F. Spray an 8-inch square baking pan with nonstick cooking spray.

2 In a medium bowl, mix together the cake mix, oil, and aquafaba until combined. Add the almond milk and mix until smooth. The batter should have a frosting-like consistency; if it seems too thick, add a little extra almond milk. Fold in the sprinkles.

3 Spread the batter in the prepared cake pan and bake until the top starts to brown and a toothpick inserted in the center comes out with moist crumbs attached, 15 to 20 minutes. Remove from the oven and let cool completely before slicing.

CRISPY LAYERED OAT BARS

Makes 8-10 bars

Having earned my degree in psychology, I'm fascinated by humans, and I enjoy the opportunity to peel back the layers that all people have. Some say that people are like onions, which also have many layers. But onions make you cry. I prefer to say that people are like these crispy layered oat bars—slightly sweet, kind of nutty, with many divine layers to dig through and enjoy.

● ● ● ●

½ cup palm shortening
¼ cup packed light brown sugar
   Pinch of salt
 1 cup rolled oats
¼ cup raisins
½ cup chocolate chips
¼ cup peanut butter
½ cup crisped rice cereal

1 Lightly spray an 8-inch-square baking pan with nonstick cooking spray.

2 Melt the shortening in a saucepan over medium heat. Once it has melted, add the brown sugar and salt and stir until the sugar begins to dissolve. Add the oats and cook, stirring constantly, for 2 to 3 minutes. Remove from the heat and stir in the raisins.

3 Press half of the oat mixture into the baking pan. Transfer the remaining half to a small bowl to reserve for the topping.

4 Add the chocolate chips to the same saucepan and melt, stirring constantly, over medium-low heat. Add the peanut butter and stir until melted together. Add the cereal and stir until evenly coated with the chocolate mixture.

5 Working quickly, spread the chocolate mixture over the oat mixture in the baking pan, pressing down firmly as you go. Spread the reserved oat mixture evenly on top of the chocolate layer, pressing down firmly.

6 Refrigerate until firm, 1 to 2 hours, before cutting into bars.

DESSERT NACHOS

Serves 2 to 4

Friends drop by at the last minute? Keep these ingredients in the cupboard and you'll always have the makings of a last-minute dessert that comes together in 10 minutes or less. Part salty, part sweet, these unconventional dessert nachos will shock and awe. Warning: Not for the faint of heart!

● ● ●●

⅓ cup vegan chocolate hazelnut butter
2½ cups mini round corn tortilla chips
¼ cup mini marshmallows
¼ cup sweetened flaked coconut

1 Preheat the broiler. Line a baking sheet with parchment paper.

2 In a small bowl, microwave the chocolate hazelnut butter until melted, 10 to 20 seconds. Stir until smooth.

3 Arrange the tortilla chips in a single layer on the baking sheet. Drizzle the chocolate hazelnut butter over the chips. Sprinkle the mini marshmallows and coconut over the top.

4 Broil until the marshmallows begin to brown, 2 to 3 minutes. Serve warm.

CHOCOLATE CHIP COOKIE CAKE PANCAKES

Makes 4 stacks

We made some crazy concoctions at my cupcake bakery. From cakes that looked like mini burgers, to "sangria and cheese" cupcakes, to sculpting people's faces out of chocolate, we liked to test the boundaries of what could be done. More often than not, the results were mind-blowingly delicious home runs. Can I just say that I think I did it again with this recipe? These stacked and jacked chocolate chip cookie + cake + pancake creations are like the rock star breakfast of your dreams. Be fierce!

1 (16-ounce) box gluten-free pancake mix

½ cup plus 2 tablespoons chocolate chips, divided

3 tablespoons plus 1 teaspoon rainbow sprinkles, divided

¼ cup Dollop Gourmet Madagascar Vanilla vegan frosting

> **note**
> ✳ ✳ ✳ ✳ ✳ ✳ ✳ ✳ ✳ ✳ ✳ ✳ ✳ ✳
> I recommend Enjoy Life Foods' pancake mix. It's vegan, gluten-free, free from the top eight allergens, and delicious.

1 Make the pancake batter according to the directions on the box. Fold ½ cup of the chocolate chips into half of the batter and 3 tablespoons of the sprinkles into the other half.

2 Spray a large frying pan with nonstick cooking spray and heat over medium heat. Working in batches, spoon ¼ cup of batter per pancake into the hot pan and cook until golden, flipping halfway through. Transfer the pancakes to a plate and repeat with the remaining batter, spraying the pan with more cooking spray as needed.

3 To assemble the stacks, lay a pancake on a plate and spread a thick layer of vanilla frosting on top. Repeat with two more pancakes, spreading vanilla frosting between each pancake. Sprinkle the remaining ½ tablespoon of chocolate chips and 1 teaspoon of sprinkles over the top. Repeat with the remaining pancakes, frosting, chocolate chips, and sprinkles. Serve warm.

APPLE PIE TAQUITOS

Makes 6 taquitos

I used to have a hot-pink Christmas tree in my bakery. Every year we would pull this bright Christmas tree from storage and place it prominently on the front table by the door. Dozens of delightful customers surprised me each winter by bringing in sparkling new cupcake ornaments to decorate the tree. Oh, you should have seen that heavenly frosted tree! My friend Jack asked for the tree when I left the bakery, and to this day he pulls it out every year at home so the tradition can live on. Jack also volunteered to test this recipe, and by the sound of his rave reviews—the taquitos didn't even survive for photos—these warm, crispy apple pie rollups will be another continuing tradition in Jack's house. I dare you to take one taste and refrain from making these a continuing tradition in your house as well. *Mmmm*, Apple Pie Taquito heaven here you come. . . .

● ● ● ●

2 apples, peeled and chopped

¾ cup water

¾ cup granulated sugar, divided

2 tablespoons cornstarch

1¼ teaspoons ground cinnamon, divided

⅛ teaspoon salt

   Coconut oil spray

6 small, soft tortillas

1 To make the apple pie filling, combine the chopped apples, water, ¼ cup of the sugar, cornstarch, ¼ teaspoon of the cinnamon, and salt in a medium saucepan and bring to a simmer over medium-low heat. Simmer the mixture, stirring occasionally, until thickened, 15 to 20 minutes. Remove from the heat and let cool while you prepare the taquito shells.

2 Preheat the oven to 350°F. Spray a 9×13-inch baking pan with the coconut oil spray.

3 In a bowl, stir together the remaining ½ cup of sugar and 1 teaspoon of cinnamon.

4 Working with one tortilla at a time, spread 1 to 2 tablespoons of the cooled apple pie filling slightly off center in the tortilla then roll up tightly. Spray the outside of the tortilla with the coconut oil spray and gently roll it in the cinnamon sugar mixture. Place in the prepared baking ban. Repeat with the remaining tortillas and filling.

5 Bake the taquitos until they start to brown, about 15 minutes. Remove from the oven and serve warm.

note
✳ ✳ ✳ ✳ ✳ ✳ ✳ ✳ ✳ ✳ ✳ ✳ ✳
If you're making these gluten-free, make sure to choose corn tortillas. You can use toothpicks to help keep the taco shells together after you roll them. By spreading the apple pie filling off center you'll help ensure the filling doesn't seep out while baking.

3 *Crazy Easy* VEGAN DESSERTS

You know those times when you're craving a healthier, tastier vegan dessert, but you want it to come together in, say, 5 minutes? Well, friend, I've got you covered. Okay, so some of the recipes in this section take 20 minutes, but I guarantee you they're all ridiculously easy to make and require few ingredients and little time. From Almond Joyish Bars (page 89) to S'mores Sandwiches (page 97) to Cherry Cheesecake Dip (page 123), your sweet tooth will be indulged quicker than you can say "gimme s'more!"

ALMOND JOYISH BARS

Makes 8

When I was a kid, my dad's favorite candy bar was the Almond Joy. But in my mind, it felt like a health food disguised in a candy costume. As a child I couldn't understand why anyone would want to eat a candy bar that was even remotely healthy. Now that I'm all grown up I've learned that the combination of almonds + coconut + chocolate is actually really tasty (in an oh-so-adult way). Enter my love for these vegan Almond Joyish Bars. Creamy almond frosting filling is enrobed in chocolate . . . my mouth is watering at the thought. All right, Dad, I'll share.

● ₀ ₍●₎ ●

½ (12-ounce) jar Dollop Gourmet Madagascar Vanilla vegan frosting

¼ teaspoon almond extract

3 tablespoons shredded unsweetened coconut, divided

¾ cup chocolate chips

note

It can take a bit of maneuvering to form the mounds here, but don't be deterred. Even if they're not the prettiest darn candies on the planet, they will be the tastiest. Mark my words. The vegan vanilla frosting of choice is Dollop Gourmet Madagascar Vanilla frosting—so rich and tasty!

1 In a small bowl, stir together the vanilla frosting, almond extract, and 2 tablespoons of the shredded coconut until well combined. Freeze the mixture until slightly firm, about 10 minutes.

2 Using a flat spatula, spread 2×1-inch mounds of the mixture on a small parchment-lined tray Place the mounds in the freezer until firm, about 10 minutes.

3 Microwave the chocolate chips at 30-second intervals, stirring in between, until melted and smooth. Slowly pour two-thirds of the melted chocolate over the mounds, spreading to coat evenly, and reserving one-third of the chocolate. Sprinkle the remaining coconut on top of the mounds. Return to the freezer until the chocolate is firm. Remove from the freezer and flip over to pour the remaining melted chocolate on the bottom of the mounds, coating evenly. Return to the freezer for the chocolate to set. Serve chilled.

PEANUT BUTTER COOKIE CUPS

Makes 8

How to one-up a peanut butter cup? Attach a chocolate chip cookie to the bottom. *Bam!* It's like having one foot in Canada and one foot in the United States—the best of both worlds. Making these treats will earn you that dual citizenship you've been dreaming of.

1 cup chocolate chips
½ cup peanut butter or peanut butter frosting
8 quarter-size vegan gluten-free chocolate chip cookies

> ### note
> Several brands make vegan mini chocolate chip cookies. Enjoy Life even makes a gluten-free vegan one. Hit your local supermarket and enjoy surveying the cookie shelves! You can make these as just plain peanut butter cups as well if you leave out the cookies.

1 Lightly spray a mini silicone cupcake pan with nonstick cooking spray.

2 Microwave the chocolate chips at 30-second intervals, stirring occasionally, until smooth and completely melted. Spread a thin layer of melted chocolate over the inside of each cup, covering the bottom and sides, using about two-thirds of the chocolate. Freeze until the chocolate is firm, about 10 minutes. Set the remaining chocolate aside.

3 Drop 1 teaspoon of peanut butter or peanut butter frosting into the center of each cup. Place 1 cookie on top of the peanut butter, pressing down so it's fully inside the cup. Repeat with the remaining cookies.

4 Spread the remaining melted chocolate over the top of each cookie to fully cover and seal the cup. Freeze the cookie cups until the chocolate is completely firm, about 15 minutes. Carefully pop out each cup from the pan and serve. Store chilled or at room temperature.

SALTED CARAMEL CHOCOLATE FUDGE

Makes 12 to 20 pieces

Every summer my family and I would spend the day at a popular amusement park not far from our home in Rochester. Waterparks, roller coasters, picnic lunch—the whole shebang. My favorite part of those adventures was not New York's oldest wooden roller coaster (and the way it made you bite your tongue every ride). No, my favorite part was the fudge shop we always visited on our way out. Rows and rows of decadent sweet fudge. My parents let us each choose a sliver of any flavor we wanted. My favorite was the salty-sweet caramel cream fudge. *Mmm*, you guys, that fudge was so dreamy....But don't take my word for it. Make this easy vegan version, and you'll see why I close my eyes and relive those summer days as often as I can.

* ● ● ●

1 (12-ounce) bag chocolate chips
1 (12-ounce) jar Dollop Gourmet Sea Salted Caramel vegan frosting
1 teaspoon coarse Himalayan sea salt

1 Line a 9-inch-square baking pan with parchment paper.

2 Microwave the chocolate chips in a medium bowl at 30-second intervals, stirring in between, until completely melted and smooth.

3 Add the frosting to the melted chocolate and stir until smooth.

4 Spread the mixture into the lined baking pan, smoothing the top. Sprinkle the sea salt over the top.

5 Cover and refrigerate until firm, about 1 hour. Cut into small squares and serve.

PEANUT BUTTER AND CHOCOLATE FUDGE

Makes 12 to 20 pieces

Yes, there are several peanut butter and chocolate recipes in this book, but that's because peanut butter and chocolate is such a winning combination! Seriously, you can't go wrong with peanut butter and chocolate anything. Having trouble making friends? Bring peanut butter and chocolate. Want to impress a date? Peanut butter and chocolate. Big review at work? Peanut butter and chocolate. This is one of the easiest peanut butter and chocolate recipes you can make. It's luscious, rich, and sure to win over any crowd, big or small.

6 tablespoons palm shortening
1 cup powdered sugar
2 tablespoons unsweetened cocoa powder
½ cup peanut butter
½ teaspoon vanilla extract
   Pinch of salt
¼ cup chocolate chips

note
You can sub almond butter for the peanut butter if that's more your style.

1 Line an 8-inch-square baking pan with parchment paper.

2 Melt the palm shortening in a saucepan over medium-low heat. Add the powdered sugar and stir well until completely combined. Stir in the cocoa powder, then add the peanut butter, vanilla, and salt, stirring until very smooth.

3 Spread the mixture into the lined baking pan, smoothing the top. Sprinkle the chocolate chips over the top.

4 Refrigerate until firm, 1 to 2 hours. Cut into small squares and serve.

DARK CHOCOLATE BARS

Makes 2 to 4

A beautiful sunset, a gentle breeze, giant adoring puppy eyes—sometimes it's the simple things in life that bring the most pleasure. Like a bar of rich, dark chocolate. Have you ever made a bar of chocolate yourself? You'll find it's so straightforward that you'll be forced to add it to that list of the simple things in life. With just a handful of ingredients and a few minutes, you'll have a decadent dark chocolate bar that rivals any of the branded ones sold in the grocery store. Just think twice before selling it to them, because that business is definitely *not* one of the simple things in life.

½ cup refined coconut oil

½ cup unsweetened dark cocoa powder, sifted

¼ cup pure maple syrup, at room temperature

2 teaspoons vanilla extract

⅛ teaspoon fine sea salt

> **note**
>
> Sprinkle chopped nuts, sprinkles, or candy on top as the chocolate sets to really make this your own.

1 Melt the coconut oil in a microwave or saucepan over medium heat.

2 Whisk in the cocoa powder, mixing until completely combined. Whisk in the maple syrup and vanilla, then add the salt and whisk until smooth.

3 Pour into a standard 2×5-inch chocolate bar mold, working in batches if necessary, or spread into two to four ½-inch-thick rectangles on a parchment-lined baking sheet. Refrigerate until firm. Keep chilled until ready to serve.

SALTED CHOCOLATE CHIP COOKIE DOUGH TRUFFLES

Makes 12

It was our second date when he surprised me with dinner at world famous Spago in Beverly Hills. It was the night before Christmas Eve, and we didn't have reservations—a real "fly by the seat of his pants" kind of guy. Fortunately, we nabbed a great people-watching table facing the center of the room. As I sat there enjoying the view, an elderly gentleman rolled in with his wife and children. The family sat at the table directly in front of us, and the waitstaff began to *fawn*. That's when we realized the man was none other than Don Rickles, the world-famous insult comic. Don Rickles reminds me of these cookie dough truffles—salty, sweet, *and* very rich—and these delightful treats are somebodies you will really want to know.

● ● ●●●

½ cup light brown sugar (not packed)
¼ cup palm shortening
2 tablespoons unsweetened almond milk
1 teaspoon vanilla extract
½ teaspoon almond extract
1 cup gluten-free flour
1½ cups chocolate chips, divided
½ teaspoon Himalayan sea salt

1 In a medium bowl, beat together the brown sugar and shortening until creamy and well combined. Add the almond milk, vanilla, and almond extract and continue mixing until well combined.

2 Slowly add the flour and continue mixing until a thick dough forms. Add half cup of the chocolate chips and mix until just combined. Roll the dough in your palms to form tablespoon-size balls.

3 Microwave the remaining 1 cup chocolate chips at 30-second intervals, stirring in between, until melted and smooth. Using a fork, dip each ball in the melted chocolate to coat completely. Place the dipped ball on a parchment-lined tray. Sprinkle lightly with sea salt. Repeat with the remaining balls and chocolate. Refrigerate until the chocolate hardens.

S'MORES SANDWICHES

Makes 6

Did you grow up eating s'mores like I did? Only in the summer and only around a campfire? Hair soaking up that smoky smell, fingers dripping with sticky marshmallow goodness? Ah, those are the memories that inspired these gooey five-minute treats! It can't always be summer, and we can't always relax around a campfire, but with a delectable jar of chocolate frosting and a handful of vegan marshmallows, we can always sit back and relax with a little bit of s'mores and a whole lot of fabulous memories.

• •• •

12 vegan graham cracker squares
¼ cup Dollop Gourmet Hot Chocolate vegan frosting
½ cup vegan marshmallow crème

note

✳ ✳ ✳ ✳ ✳ ✳ ✳ ✳ ✳ ✳ ✳

Vegan marshmallow crème called Ricemellow Creme can be found at most natural food stores or online.

1 Arrange 6 graham crackers upside down on a work surface. Spread the chocolate frosting evenly over the graham crackers.

2 Arrange the remaining 6 graham crackers upside down on the work surface. Spread the marshmallow crème evenly over the graham crackers.

3 Press a chocolate-frosted graham cracker against a marshmallow-covered graham cracker so the chocolate and marshmallow sides are touching. Squeeze gently so the halves stick together. Repeat with the remaining graham crackers. Serve at once.

BIRTHDAY GLITTER BOMBS

Makes 9

Is it weird for me to say these Birthday Glitter Bombs remind me of Miley Cyrus? Or maybe they're more Mariah Carey. Either way, these cake batter–flavored cookie dough balls rolled in sparkling colorful sugar are amazing, beautiful, and the real deal. Actually, when I put it that way, they don't really remind me of Miley *or* Mariah anymore . . .

¼ cup palm shortening
⅓ cup granulated sugar
2 tablespoons packed light brown sugar
1½ teaspoons vanilla extract
½ cup gluten-free flour
Pinch of salt
1 to 2 teaspoons unsweetened almond milk
2 tablespoons vegan rainbow sprinkles
2 tablespoons Dollop Gourmet Madagascar Vanilla vegan frosting
2 tablespoons rainbow sanding sugar

note

I used Bob's Red Mill 1-to-1 Gluten-Free Flour. This recipe works just as well with regular flour if you don't need to eat gluten-free. Try different colored sprinkles and sanding sugar for different occasions.

1 In a medium bowl, mix the vegetable shortening, sugars, and vanilla until well blended. Slowly add the flour and salt and mix until combined. Add enough almond milk until the dough comes together and can be easily rolled. Fold in the sprinkles. Refrigerate the dough for 10 minutes to firm up.

2 Roll a tablespoon-size portion of dough into a ball, then flatten it between your fingers. Drop ¼ teaspoon vanilla frosting in the middle of the dough, then fold the dough around the frosting to enclose it and roll into a ball. Roll the ball in sanding sugar to coat and place on a parchment-lined tray. Repeat with the remaining dough, frosting, and sanding sugar. Refrigerate until ready to serve.

CHOCOLATE-DIPPED
ALMOND BUTTER–STUFFED
PRETZELS

Makes 12

I held 30-some jobs before I turned 24, several of them in offices. I learned that working in an office makes me hungry, especially around 3 p.m. or so. Does this happen to you, too? Well, these chocolate-dipped almond butter-stuffed pretzels are the perfect sweet but healthy snack for you to make at home and start munching on when that craving strikes. Make a few extra—your coworkers *will* beg you for some.

• • •

¼ cup almond butter
24 mini pretzel twists
1 cup chocolate chips

note

Try sprinkling the tops with vegan sprinkles before the chocolate sets for an extra festive snack.

1 Spread 1 teaspoon of almond butter on one side of 1 pretzel. Top with another pretzel, pressing together gently so they stick. Repeat with the remaining pretzels and almond butter to make 12 sandwiches total.

2 Microwave the chocolate in a small bowl at 30-second intervals, stirring in between, until melted and smooth.

3 Holding a pretzel sandwich with your fingers, dip three-quarters of the sandwich into the melted chocolate, turning to coat both sides. Place on a parchment-lined plate. Repeat with the remaining pretzel sandwiches and chocolate and let set before serving.

MEXICAN HOT COCOA PARTY MIX

Serves 8 to 10

Did you grow up seeing Muddy Buddies at every holiday party like I did? Christmas Muddy Buddies, Easter Muddy Buddies, Halloween Muddy Buddies—it's the chameleon of snack mixes. You can make a mix to suit any occasion. Seriously, try it. One of my favorites though is the occasion of hanging out in front of a toasty fire on a blustery winter day. And for that occasion, this chocolaty mix is the perfect soul-warming treat.

1 cup vegan instant hot cocoa mix

2 teaspoons ground cinnamon

¾ cup chocolate chips

6 cups Rice Chex cereal

1 cup mini marshmallows

note
✳ ✳ ✳ ✳ ✳ ✳ ✳ ✳ ✳ ✳ ✳ ✳ ✳
Not all hot cocoa mixes are vegan, but many are. Check those labels, and you're sure to easily find one or more at your local store.

1 Combine the cocoa mix and cinnamon in a large resealable plastic bag and mix well.

2 Microwave the chocolate in a medium bowl at 30-second intervals, stirring in between, until completely melted and smooth.

3 Mix together the cereal and marshmallows in a large bowl. Pour the melted chocolate over the mix and toss until evenly coated.

4 Pour the coated cereal into the cocoa and cinnamon and shake bag until everything is evenly coated.

CHOCOLATE BANANA PEANUT BUTTER POPCORN

Serves 1 to 2

Popcorn is one of my all-time favorite snacks. Maybe it's because I grew up watching my mom eat it for dinner on busy nights, or because when my grandma took us to see movies she snuck a bag of half-burnt popcorn into her purse. Popcorn is light, portable, and the perfect vehicle for loads of delicious toppings, like chocolate chips, banana chips, and peanuts. Toss them in, shake the bag, and you've got yourself the perfect snack or accompaniment for that special flick.

• • • •

1 bag (4–5 ounces) plain or lightly salted popped popcorn
¾ cup chopped salted or unsalted peanuts
¾ cup banana chips
¾ cup chocolate chips

note
✳ ✳ ✳ ✳ ✳ ✳ ✳ ✳ ✳ ✳ ✳ ✳
This is a great snack mix for that next get-together, game night, or kids' sleepover.

1 Line two baking sheets with parchment paper. Divide the popcorn evenly over each sheet. Sprinkle the peanuts and banana chips evenly over the popcorn.

2 Microwave the chocolate chips in a small bowl at 30-second intervals, stirring in between, until completely melted and smooth.

3 Drizzle the melted chocolate evenly over the popcorn mixture. Let cool to firm up (you can refrigerate the baking sheets to speed up the process). Once the chocolate is firm, transfer the popcorn to a bowl and serve.

ORANGE ALMOND COOKIES

Makes 12 to 14 cookies

I love to work out. I've been hitting the gym five to seven mornings a week for more than 10 years now. It's part of my morning routine, just like brushing my teeth. Lifting weights is what I get really pumped about, the heavier the better. And with all this heavy lifting, I feel like I can eat more cookies, like these healthy, protein-packed cookies bursting with maple syrup and ground almonds. A couple of these bad boys pre- or post-lift are certain to help you get #allthegainz.

1 cup almond flour
1 cup oat flour
½ cup pure maple syrup
½ teaspoon orange extract
½ teaspoon almond extract

note

Sprinkle the cookies with a pinch of coarse turbinado sugar before baking for a little extra crunch and sweetness.

1 Preheat the oven to 350°F. Line a baking sheet with parchment paper.

2 In a medium bowl, mix together all ingredients until well combined. Arrange tablespoon-size balls of dough on the lined baking sheet. Flatten each ball slightly to form ¼-inch-thick cookies.

3 Bake until the edges begin to brown, 12 to 15 minutes. Let cool completely before removing from the baking sheet.

MINT CUPS

Makes 8

My grandma liked to take us to Olive Garden, her favorite restaurant. She loved the unlimited salad with extra black olives and chicken parm. Me? I just went for those bite-size mint chocolate candies they served with the check. I knew they gave one per person, but I couldn't help sneaking more than my share. The creamy mint filling inside these homemade chocolate candy cups brings back fond memories of those meals with my one-of-a-kind grandma.

1 cup chocolate chips
½ cup Dollop Gourmet Madagascar Vanilla vegan frosting
¼ teaspoon crème de menthe extract
2 drops green food coloring (optional)

note

This is the perfect treat for St. Patrick's Day! You can find all-natural food coloring in your local natural foods store or online.

1 Lightly spray a mini silicone cupcake pan with nonstick cooking spray.

2 Microwave the chocolate chips at 30-second intervals, stirring in between, until smooth and completely melted. Spread a thin layer of melted chocolate over the inside of each cup, covering the bottom and sides, using about two-thirds of the chocolate. Freeze until the chocolate is firm, about 10 minutes. Set the remaining chocolate aside.

3 In a small bowl, mix together the vanilla frosting, crème de menthe, and green food coloring, if using, until well blended.

4 Remove the pan from the freezer and scoop 1½ teaspoons of the frosting mixture into the center of each cup.

5 Spread the remaining melted chocolate over the frosting mixture to fully cover and seal each cup. Freeze the cookie cups until the chocolate is completely firm, about 15 minutes. Carefully pop out each cup from the pan and serve. Store chilled or at room temperature.

APPLE CUT-OUT "COOKIES"

Serves 2 to 4

Every month for more than two years I went on my local television news station to show viewers how to make easy delicious desserts, and every minute was a blast. This apple cut-out "cookie" recipe, from one of my back-to-school segments, makes the perfect after-school treat. Kids love to frost and decorate these apple slices, which offer a healthier alternative to traditional cookie bases.

4 medium apples
1 cup peanut butter frosting
½ (12-ounce) jar Dollop Gourmet Sea Salted Caramel vegan frosting
¼ cup unsweetened shredded coconut
¼ cup mini chocolate chips
¼ cup sprinkles

1 Wash, pat dry, and core the apples. Cut lengthwise into ¼-inch-thick slices. Arrange the slices on a tray for decorating.

2 Frost the top of each slice with the peanut butter frosting or caramel frosting as you would a sugar cookie. Sprinkle any combination of coconut, chocolate chips, and sprinkles over the cookies and eat at once.

> **note**
> ✳ ✳ ✳ ✳ ✳ ✳ ✳ ✳ ✳ ✳ ✳
> Let the kids frost and decorate the apple slices themselves. It's a real interactive creative treat!

CINNAMON CREAM CHEESE-STUFFED DATES

Makes 12 dates

Did you know I was on *Steve Harvey*? Good God, I hope you didn't see it. The show's topic was "I'm Too Picky and Can't Find a Man." The producers dressed me in a bright red dress and heels I couldn't walk in (literally, I could not walk in them), and Steve proceeded to list all my "dating specifications" to an audience full of booing women. When I say it was embarrassing, I'm not exaggerating. I mean, yes, I have a lot of preferences when it comes to dating, as every lady should! I know what I like and what I don't like in a date. But there's nothing wrong with that, and one day it will pay off when I find the most fabulous man. But you know what I truly love in a date? Sweet cream cheese, cinnamon, and walnuts. Now, if Steve Harvey had brought out one of these delicious stuffed dates for me (instead of that guy from Washington, DC), I would be singing his praises and thanking the producers for upgrading my life.

● ●●

12 Medjool dates

4 ounces plain vegan cream cheese, softened

½ teaspoon ground cinnamon

2 tablespoons powdered sugar (optional)

¼ cup chopped walnuts

note

Try serving these as an appetizer instead of dessert!

1 Slice each date lengthwise, but only halfway through. Remove the pit and discard.

2 In a small bowl, mix the cream cheese with the cinnamon and sugar, if using, until soft and very creamy. Spoon ½ tablespoon of the cream cheese mixture into each date and arrange on a plate. Sprinkle with chopped walnuts and serve.

BANANA PEANUT BUTTER COOKIES TO SHARE WITH YOUR PUP

Makes 10 cookies

Donald is a 25-pound rescue mutt and the furry little love of my life. We've driven cross-country together, stayed in many hotels, flown back across the country, lived in L.A. and NYC, climbed mountains in Colorado, been on TV sets, shopped in grocery stores, shared desserts . . . yes, we've done it all. Speaking of shared desserts, this is Donald's all-time favorite homemade cookie. With creamy peanut butter and mashed banana, he can't resist. The best part, though, is that these are tasty and healthy for you to eat as well. What's better than sharing cookies with your pup? Nothing!

2 ripe bananas, mashed
1 cup rolled oats
⅓ cup creamy peanut butter
½ teaspoon vanilla extract

note

If you make this these cookies and share them with your pup, make sure to Instagram and Snapchat the occasion. Tag your pic #VeryEasyVeganDogs.

1 Preheat the oven to 350°F. Line a baking sheet with parchment paper.

2 In a medium bowl, mix all ingredients together until well blended. Arrange tablespoon-size balls of dough on the lined baking sheet and flatten slightly.

3 Bake until slightly golden, 12 to 15 minutes. Remove from the oven and let cool completely before sharing with your pup.

WINE-ROASTED CINNAMON PEARS

Serves 4

What's your favorite fruit? Mine must be pears. There's something about their sweet graininess that gets me all jazzed up. Usually I like my pears as crunchy as an apple, but when they're soft and roasted, their flavor and texture pop in a most desirable way. Add my favorite thing—wine!—and you get one devilish dessert.

4 medium ripe-but-firm pears, quartered and seeded

¼ cup red or white wine

2 tablespoons packed light brown sugar

½ teaspoon ground cinnamon

2 cups vegan vanilla ice cream (optional)

note
* * * * * * * * * * * *
Having a dinner party or date night? This sophisticated and romantic dessert will knock your people's socks off. Just make sure that's the vibe you're going for first!

1 Preheat the oven to 400°F. Line a small roasting pan with foil.

2 Place the pears in the roasting pan. In a small bowl, stir together the wine, brown sugar, and cinnamon. Pour the wine mixture evenly over the pears and toss to coat.

3 Roast until tender, 20 to 30 minutes. Remove from the oven and serve warm with a scoop of ice cream, if you like.

STRAWBERRY CHOCOLATE CHIA TOASTS

Serves 4

If you haven't tried dessert on toast, you're totally missing out. Just think of toast as a blank canvas that you can adorn however you desire. Let the creativity flow! Start with a "paint" of sweet sauce, frosting, or jam and add toppings from there. Here, the vibrant flavor of fresh strawberries pairs well with sweet chocolate frosting, while a sprinkling of chia seeds adds a crunchy nutritional burst. Your edible art is ready to be devoured!

4 slices bread

4 tablespoons Dollop Gourmet Hot Chocolate vegan frosting

4 large strawberries, hulled and sliced

4 teaspoons chia seeds

1 Toast the bread until golden brown. Arrange on a work surface.

2 Spread 1 tablespoon of chocolate frosting on each toast. Arrange the sliced strawberries over the frosting. Sprinkle 1 teaspoon of chia seeds over each toast. Serve immediately.

note

There're so many desserts you can make on toast! Experiment with other spreads, fruits, and toppings. Try vegan caramel sauce with a topping of roasted sweet potatoes. Or try vegan vanilla frosting with sugar cookie pieces and a smattering of rainbow sprinkles for a unique birthday cake–style treat.

BANANA SPLIT ICE CREAM

Serves 2 to 4

It was only on the most special of occasions that we'd go out for ice cream and my mom would get a banana split. We'd all take a taste of that ginormous sundae and *ooh* and *ahh* over how decadent it was. This vegan banana split, while decidedly healthier, tastes just as amazingly creamy and good as the ones I grew up on. No need to save this for special occasions though—it takes just minutes to whip up and even fewer to devour.

2 large ripe bananas, frozen

⅓ cup unsweetened almond milk

1 teaspoon vanilla extract

1½ teaspoons unsweetened dark cocoa powder

¼ cup chocolate chips

½ cup sliced fresh strawberries

Sprinkles (optional)

Maraschino cherries (optional)

1 In a food processor, process the frozen bananas with the almond milk and vanilla until smooth and creamy; the mixture should resemble soft serve ice cream. Add the cocoa powder and process until fully incorporated.

2 Scoop the ice cream into dishes. Top with chocolate chips and sliced strawberries. Add sprinkles and a cherry on top, if you like.

note
* * * * * * * * * * * *
The ice cream tastes best when it's freshly made. If you store it in the freezer, let it sit on the counter for 5 minutes or so to soften before eating.

PEANUT BUTTER CUP ICE CREAM

Serves 2 to 4

The woman who tested this recipe for me hates bananas, but much to her surprise (and mine) she loved this creamy frozen treat! The bananas take such a backseat that she barely even noticed them here. Super easy to make, this recipe is perfect on a hot summer day, a cold wintry night, or just because you need that ice cream fix. As a matter of fact, I'm going to go make myself a batch right now!

• •••

2 large ripe bananas, frozen
⅓ cup unsweetened almond milk
1 teaspoon vanilla extract
1½ tablespoons unsweetened dark cocoa powder
¼ cup peanut butter

1 Combine the frozen bananas, almond milk, and vanilla in a food processor and process until creamy and smooth; the mixture should resemble soft serve ice cream. Add the cocoa powder and process until fully incorporated. Add the peanut butter and continue mixing until smooth.

2 Scoop the ice cream into dishes and serve at once.

note
✳ ✳ ✳ ✳ ✳ ✳ ✳ ✳ ✳ ✳ ✳
The ice cream tastes best when it's freshly made. If you store it in the freezer, let it sit on the counter for 5 minutes or so to soften before eating. Like your ice cream extra chocolatey? An extra tablespoon of dark cocoa powder never hurt anyone!

FROZEN HOT CHOCOLATE

Serves 1

One of my favorite words is *serendipity*, meaning fortunate discoveries made by accident. To me, serendipity means that anything is possible and that life will always pleasantly surprise you when you least expect it. These serendipities are precisely what make life so much fun. I also love the movie *Serendipity* and have watched it dozens of times. Some of the film takes place at a famous New York institution, a lovely little café called Serendipity 3, famous for its oversize frozen hot chocolate. I love the idea of serendipity so much that I got a tattoo of this frozen hot chocolate on the back of my neck to remind myself that life can always pleasantly surprise me.

• • • • •

1 cup ice cubes
1 cup vanilla or chocolate almond milk
1 packet instant hot cocoa mix
¼ cup vegan whipped cream

Combine the ice, almond milk, and hot cocoa mix in a blender and blend until smooth. Pour into a glass and top with the vegan whipped cream.

note

Try adding a little vodka
to warm your soul!

RUM ROOT BEER FLOAT

Makes 1 float

To this day I still love root beer. I rarely drink it anymore because they say pop is *bad*, but sometimes you must indulge. Best way? Throw in some ice cream and rum and savor yourself a rum root beer float. Oh, the *badness*!

1 (12-ounce) bottle or can of root beer
2 ounces spiced rum
2 scoops vegan vanilla ice cream
¼ cup vegan whipped cream (optional)
1 maraschino cherry (optional)

Pour the root beer into a tall glass. Add the rum and stir gently to combine. Add the ice cream. Top with whipped cream and a cherry, if you like, and enjoy!

note

Skip the rum to make these alcohol-free for children! Try with cream soda for a different spin. Or if you really want your mind blown, combine vegan vanilla ice cream, grape soda, and a peanut butter sauce swirl to bring your pb&j desires into float heaven.

ORANGE CREAM SHAKE

Makes 1 shake

The Irondequoit Mall was a beautiful mall built in my hometown of Rochester, New York, when I turned eight. The mall had two levels, and the ceiling was made almost entirely of glass. These days, it sits vacant and destroyed inside, but let's not make this story sad right now. I remember hanging at that mall with my friends, gossiping about boys, stopping in the science store for glow-in-the-dark stars, and sitting on the benches sipping from large white cups of Orange Julius. This foamy sweet orange beverage brings back all the best childhood memories. Make this copycat shake right now and start sipping on the good times.

2 scoops vegan vanilla ice cream
1½ cups orange juice
½ cup vanilla almond milk

Combine the ice cream, orange juice, and almond milk in a blender and blend until smooth. Pour into a glass and enjoy at once.

note
✳ ✳ ✳ ✳ ✳ ✳ ✳ ✳ ✳ ✳ ✳ ✳
Try with other juices for a twist. Cranberry juice, pineapple juice . . . even a mixture of the two! Sub chocolate ice cream if that chocolate + orange combo is what your dreams are made of.

CHERRY CHEESECAKE DIP

Serves 8 to 10

My *Shark Tank* viewing party was truly a magical night. All of my friends, family, and business acquaintances gathered in a large room on the second floor of the flagship Wegmans to watch what happened when I appeared on the hit show, pitching my company, Dollop Gourmet. Dozens of chairs were set up in front of a large-screen TV, and another large TV was positioned near the bar. The highlight, aside from the eruption of cheers when my face appeared on the screen, was the frosting bar I had set up—an 18-foot table arrayed with frosting dips, pretzels, chips, fruit, sprinkles, marshmallows, cookies . . . you name it. This frosting bar was stacked! People made their way along the bar, dipping and dolloping their own sweet creations. Sweet dips really add some life to a party! Take this cherry cheesecake dip, for example. Paired with cookies or graham crackers, this cherry cheesecake–flavored dip will bring life and sparkle to any occasion.

• • ••

8 ounces vegan cream cheese

6 ounces vegan yogurt

2 teaspoons vanilla extract

½ cup powdered sugar

1 (21-ounce) can cherry pie filling
Vegan cookies or graham crackers
for dipping

1 Mix the cream cheese in the bowl of a stand mixer until smooth. Add the yogurt and vanilla and mix until well combined. Slowly add the powdered sugar and whip until smooth.

2 Spoon the cheesecake mixture into a bowl. Spread the cherries evenly over the top. Serve with cookies or graham crackers for dipping.

note

There are so many vegan yogurts on the shelves these days. Some made with cashews, some with almonds, some with soy. Pick your favorite!

IRISH CREAM COOKIE DIP

Serves 12

We used to make Guinness® & Baileys™ cupcakes every St. Patrick's Day and Father's Day at my bakery in New York. They were a massive hit. Put a slug of alcohol in your dessert and the crowd goes bananas! Lucky for you, I've created this Irish Cream Cookie Dip based on inspiration from those cupcakes. It's a real crowd pleaser. This dip is ten times easier to make and—dare I say— maybe twice as delicious.

8 ounces vegan cream cheese

½ cup powdered sugar

¼ cup vegan Irish cream, preferably Bailey's Almande™

½ cup mini chocolate chips

Vegan cookies, for dipping

1 In a medium bowl, cream together the cream cheese and powdered sugar until smooth and fluffy. Add the Irish cream and mix until smooth. Stir in the chocolate chips.

2 Serve in a bowl with vegan cookies for dipping.

> **note**
>
> Chocolate chip cookies are my favorite to serve with this recipe.

CHOCOLATE RASPBERRY PUDDING PARFAITS

Makes 4 parfaits

Prior to making these parfaits, it had been years since I'd eaten instant pudding. With all the artificial and chemical junk in it, instant pudding just didn't have a place in my life. But then one day I walked down the pudding aisle of the grocery store and was struck by a craving for creamy, thick chocolate pudding that fills your mouth and goes down cold and smooth . . . I missed that unique sensation! So I stood there staring at the packages, fighting my intense craving, when there it was: natural, no-artificial-anything *chocolate pudding mix.* Shut *up*! I swiftly grabbed three pouches, a carton of unsweetened almond milk, a pint of raspberries, and practically jogged all the way home. And boy, am I glad I did! So if you, my friend, have a hankering for pudding (and how could you not?), put your bib on and dive right in to these natural vegan delights.

• • • •

1 cup cold unsweetened almond milk

1 (3.9-ounce) packet natural vegan chocolate pudding mix

2 cups fresh raspberries

NOTE

* * * * * * * * * * * * *

Jell-o® brand Simply Good Chocolate pudding mix is my pudding of choice. Make sure to whisk well and add the milk slowly, or you will end up with lumpy pudding.

1 Make the pudding by whisking the almond milk into the pudding mix until smooth.

2 Scoop some of the pudding into four glasses and top with a few raspberries. Continue alternating layers of pudding and raspberries until glasses are filled. Serve chilled.

ACKNOWLEDGMENTS

To Dollop fans, followers, and supporters—thank you! Without you, none of this would exist.

To my family, thank you for supporting my dreams and encouraging my ambitions.

To Adam, thank you for believing in me.

And to my fab recipe testers—Jack Porcello, Caitlin and John Loury, Nancy Yingling, and Mitchie Curran. Thank you for testing and ultimately loving these recipes!

Lastly, to the magical cities of Los Angeles and New York City—your inspirational backdrops aided in the creation of this masterpiece.

ABOUT THE AUTHOR

HEATHER SAFFER, founder and CEO of Dollop Gourmet, is the creator of the world's tastiest vegan gourmet frostings and snacks, all made from premium non-GMO and gluten-free ingredients. In 2012, Saffer competed on Food Network's nationally acclaimed competition show Cupcake Wars, bringing home the crown and catapulting Dollop Gourmet into the national spotlight. With her entrepreneurial spirit, Saffer then reformulated her bakery's frostings for everyday use, launching Dollop Gourmet into over 600 grocery and retail outlets. Her line of vegan frostings and snacks can now be found in Whole Foods and Wegmans and at other top retailers and markets nationwide, as well as on Amazon. In May 2016, Saffer and Dollop Gourmet were featured on ABC's hit show Shark Tank. Saffer has also been featured in *Forbes, People*, the *Huffington Post, USA Today, Women's World, Oprah*, and Yummly, among others. She currently resides in Los Angeles with her furry best friend, Donald.

IMAGE CREDITS

Food photography by Bill Milne;

iStock: © Julie Melon (object icons); © MichikoDesign (dog); © Alan Uster (borders)

INDEX